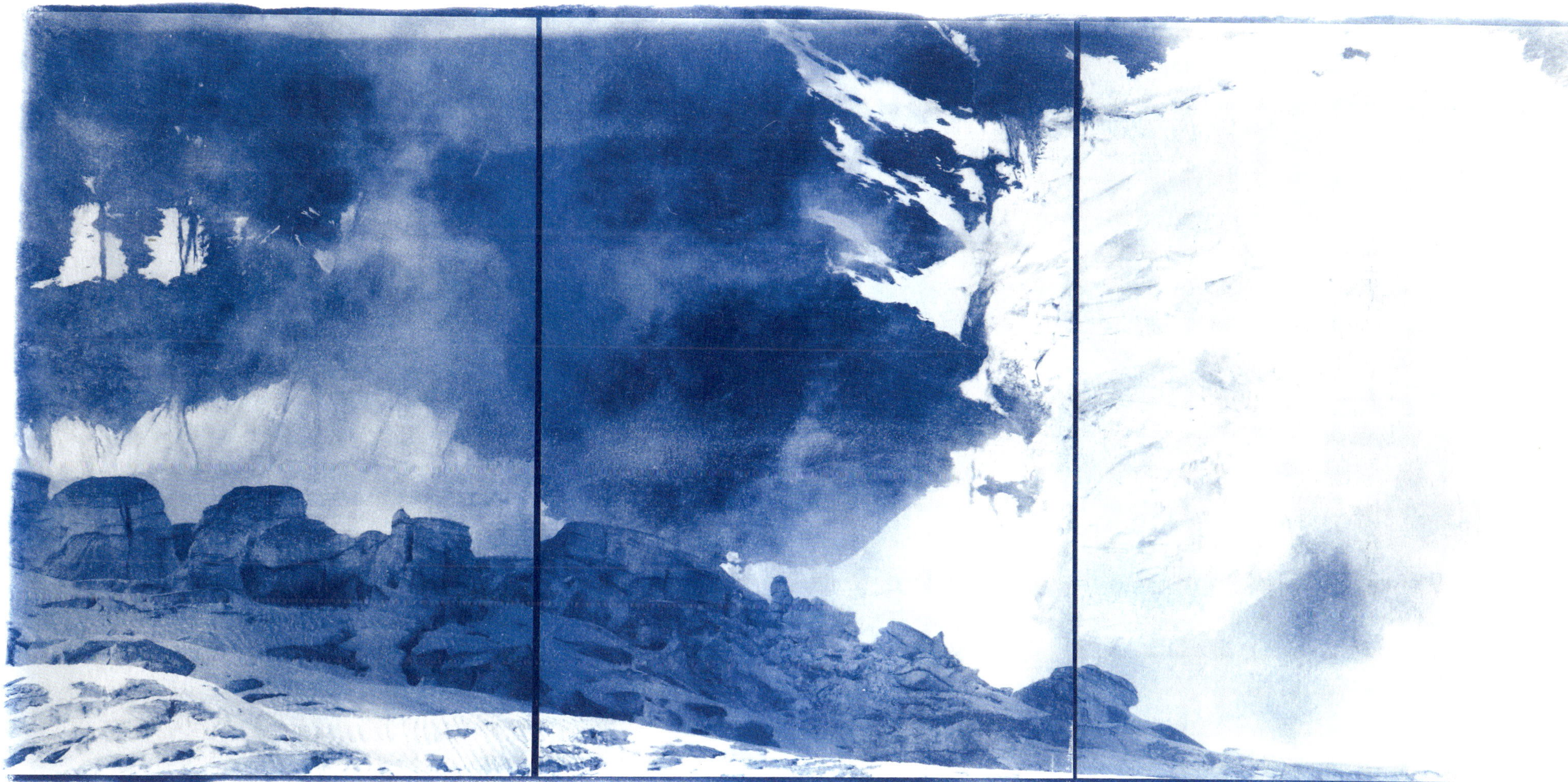

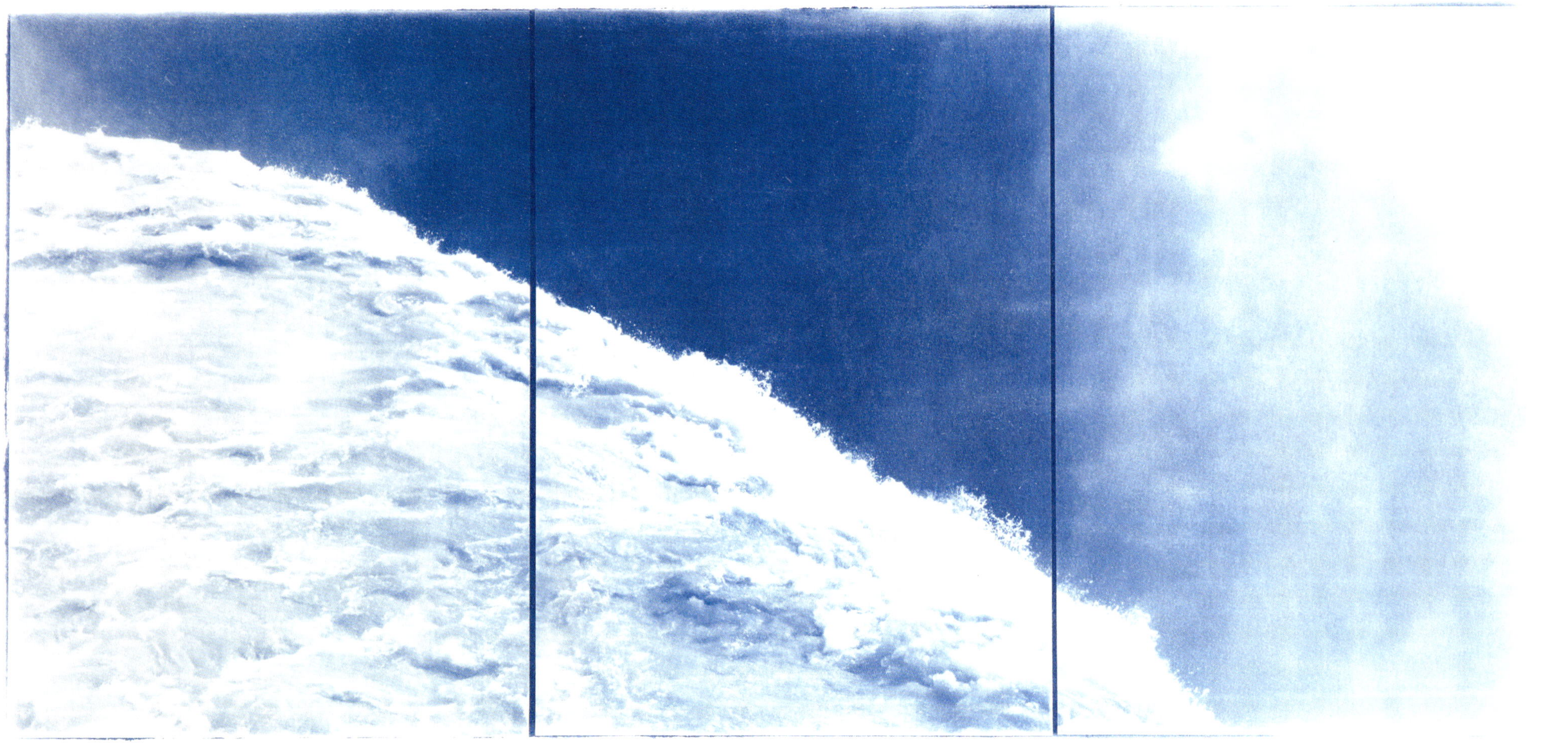

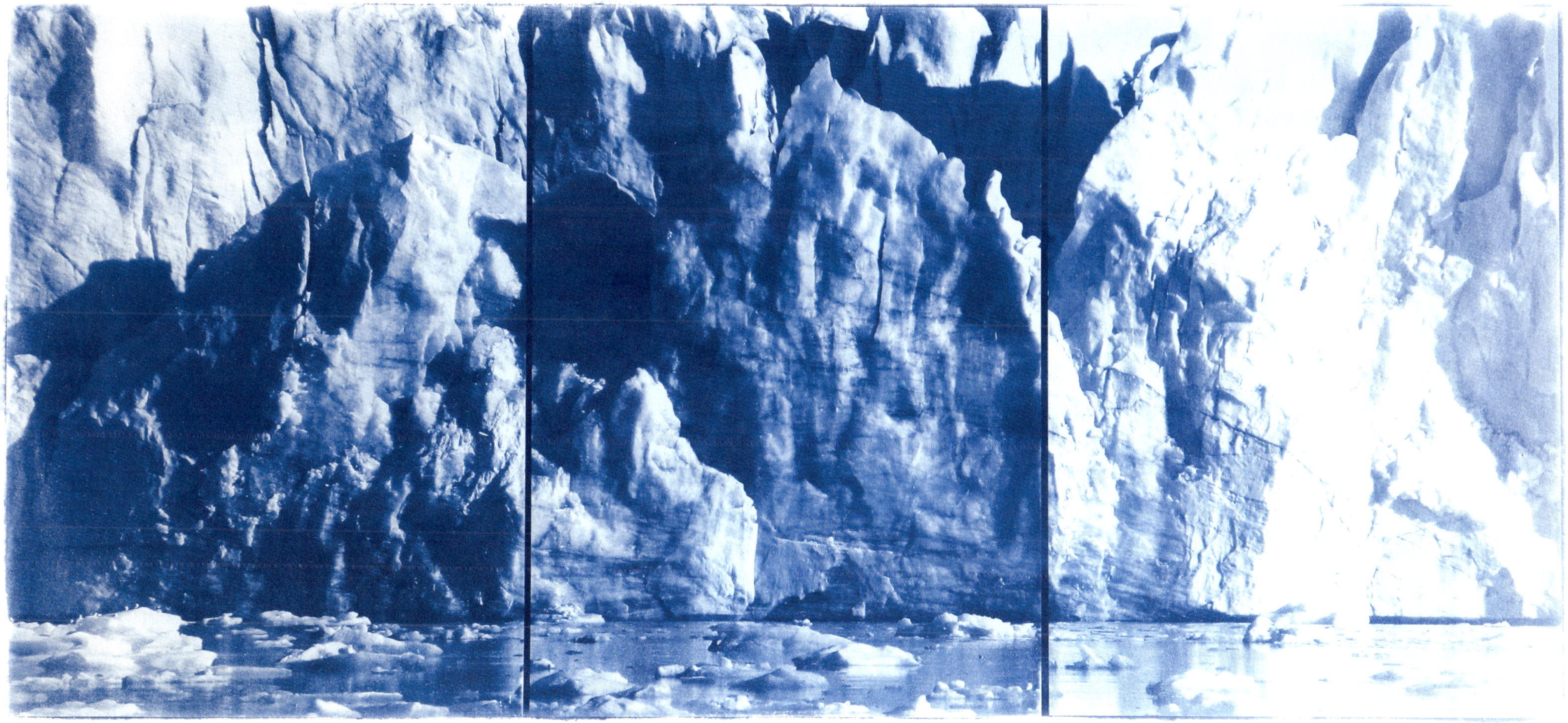

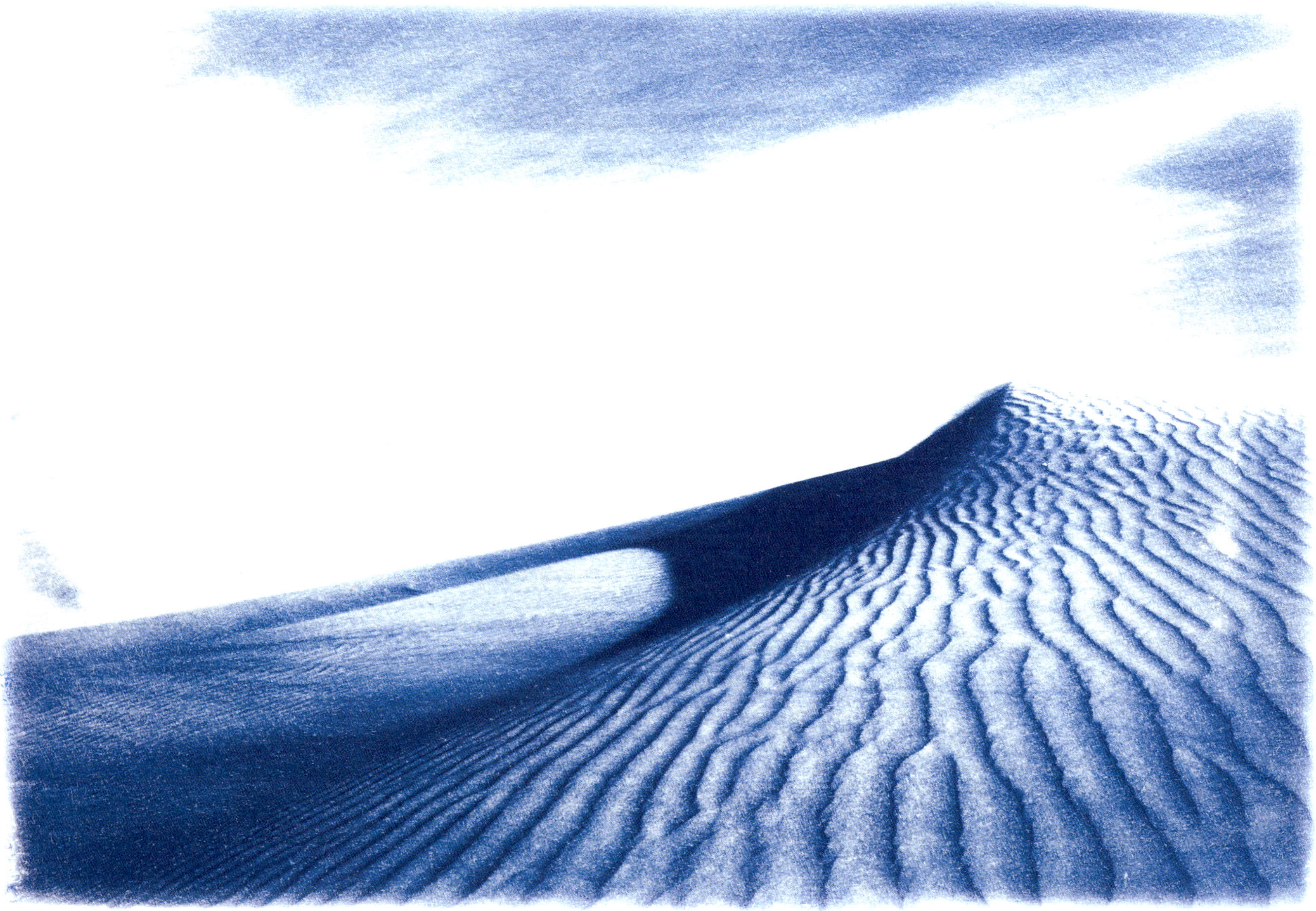

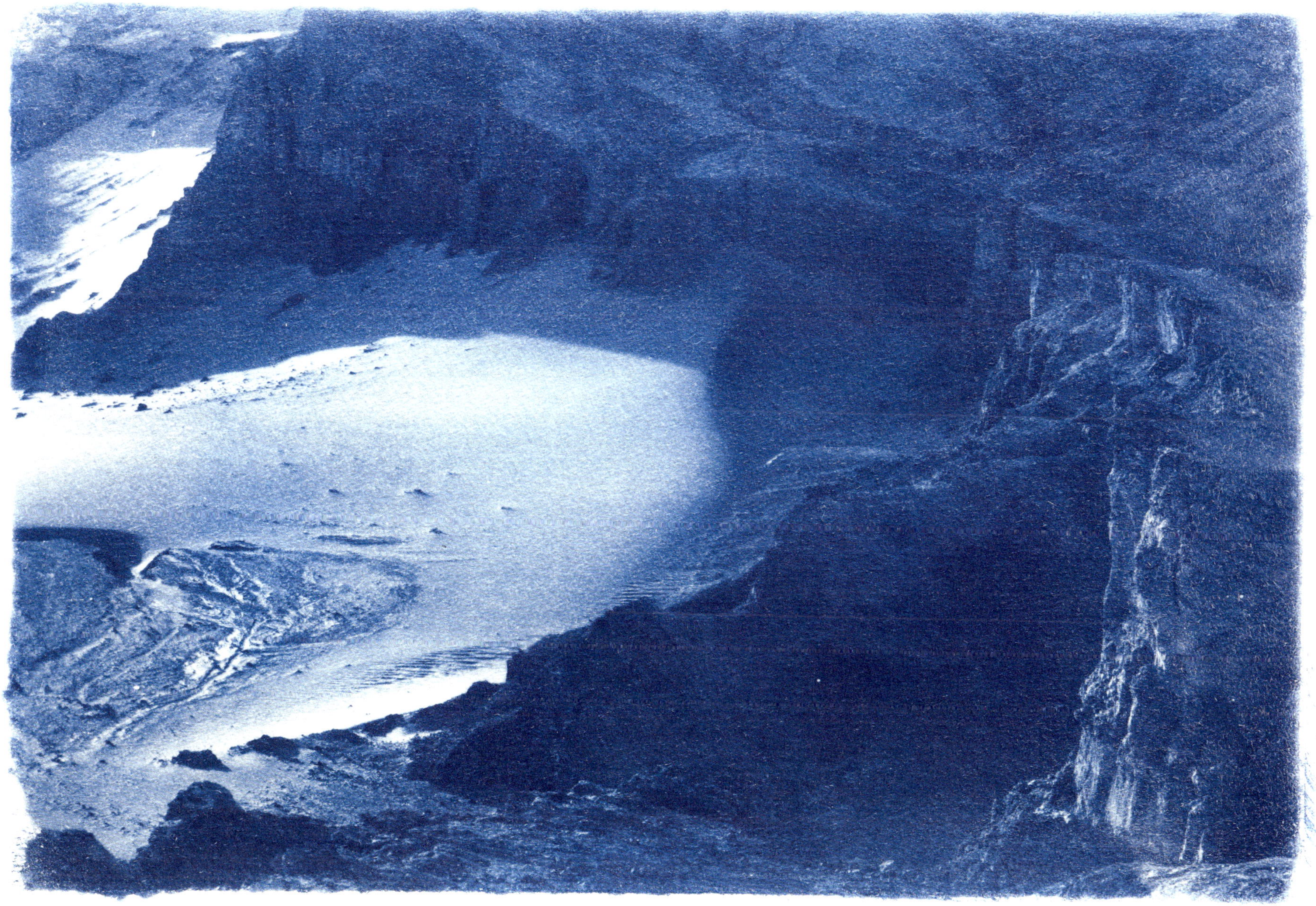

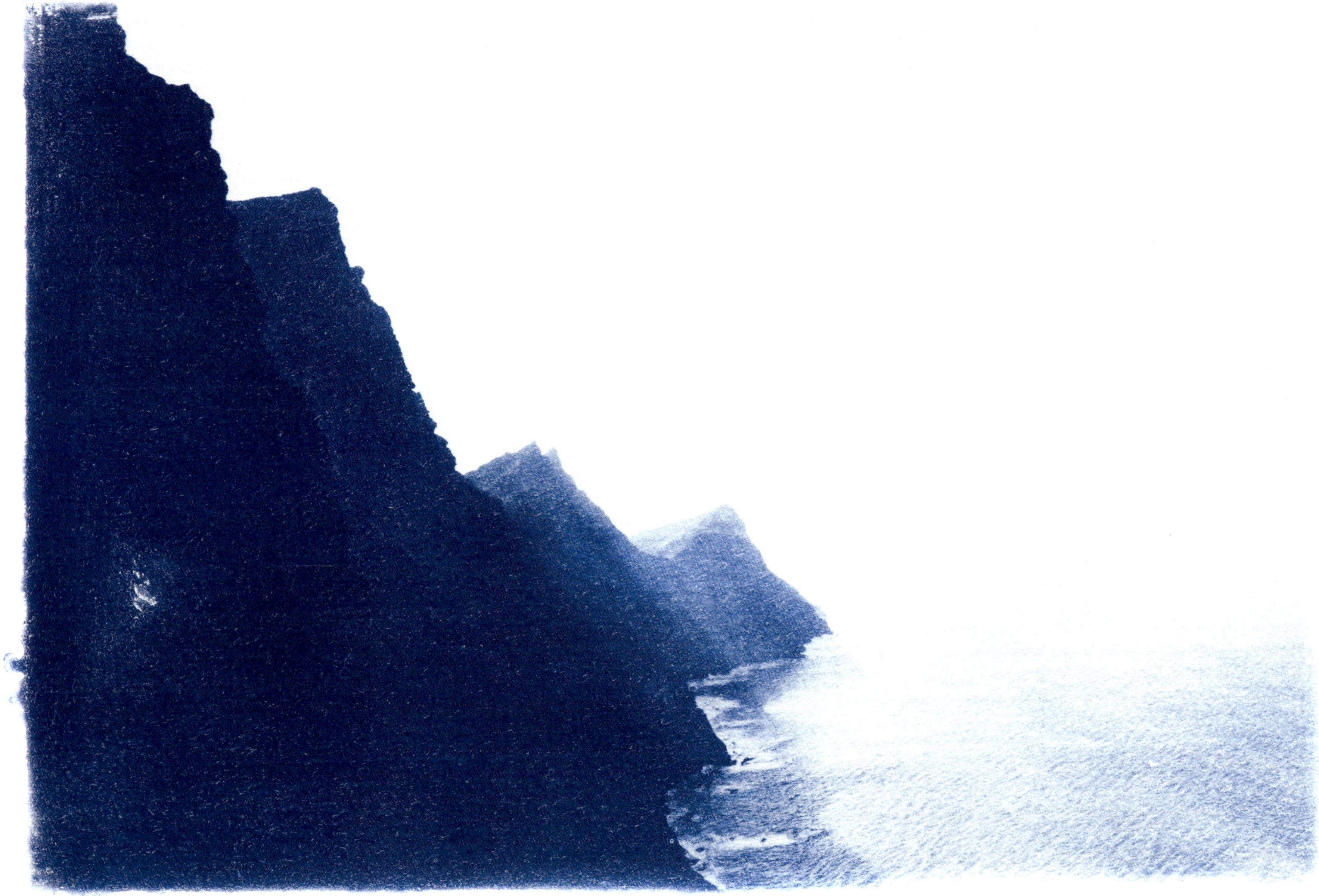

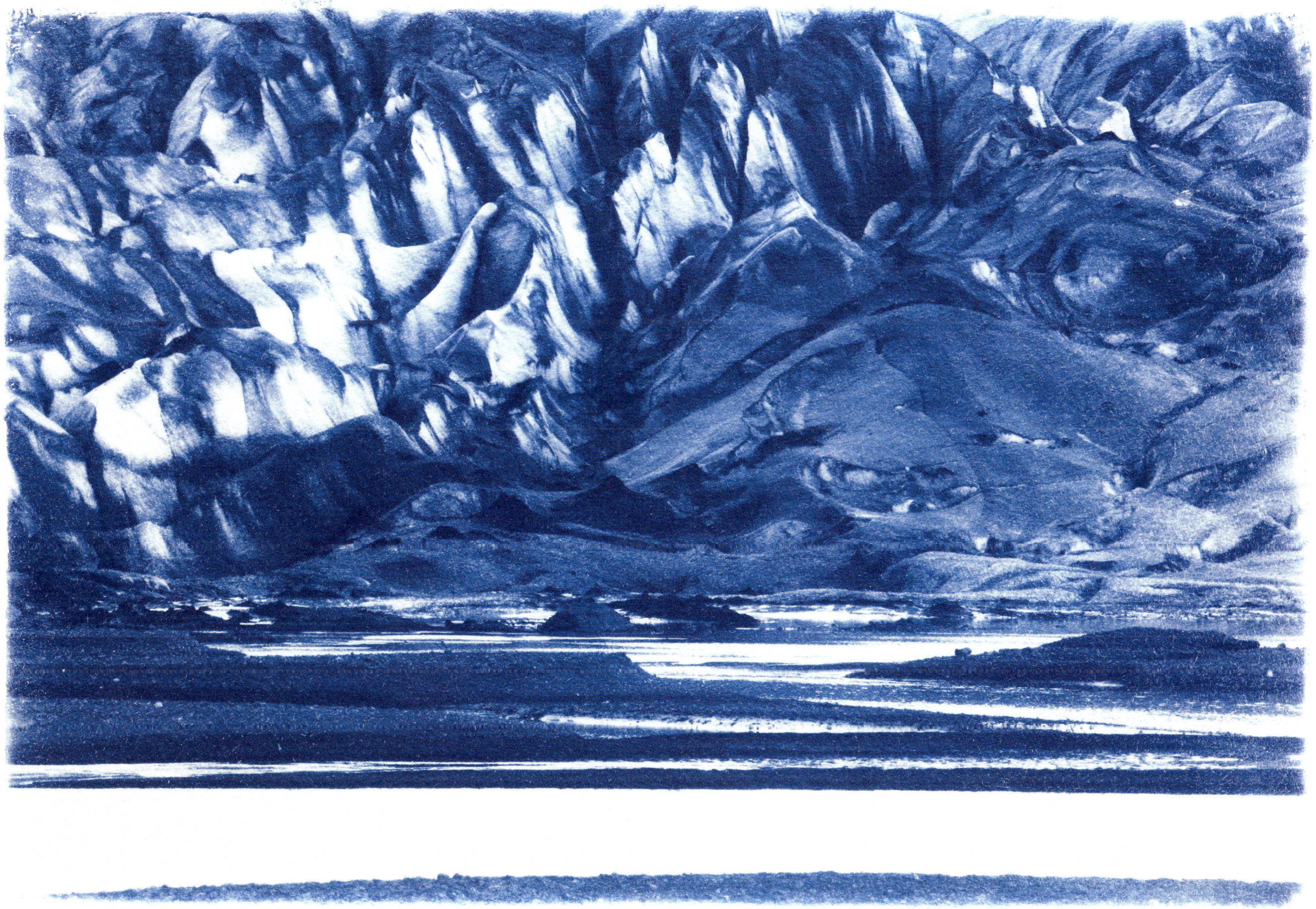

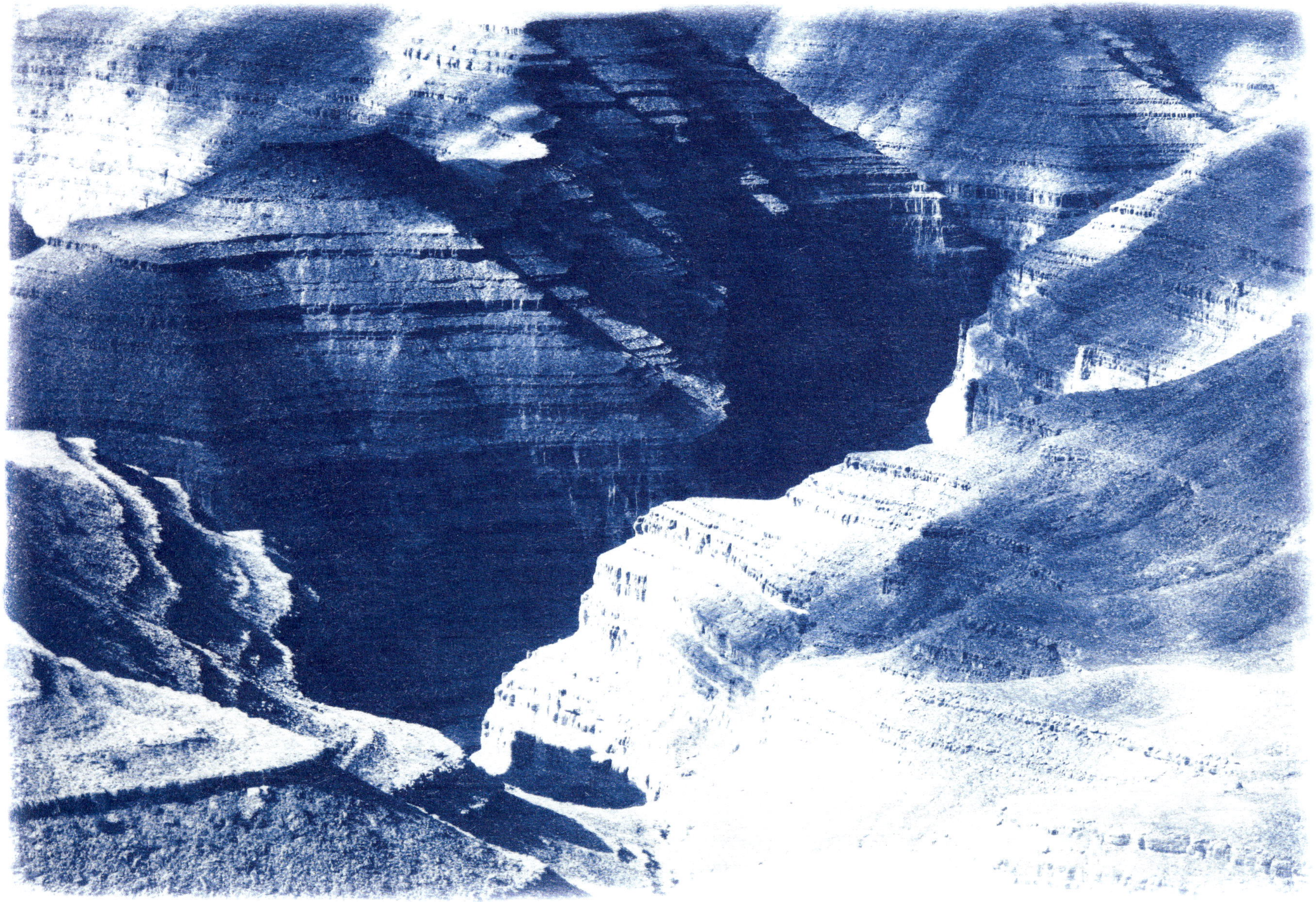

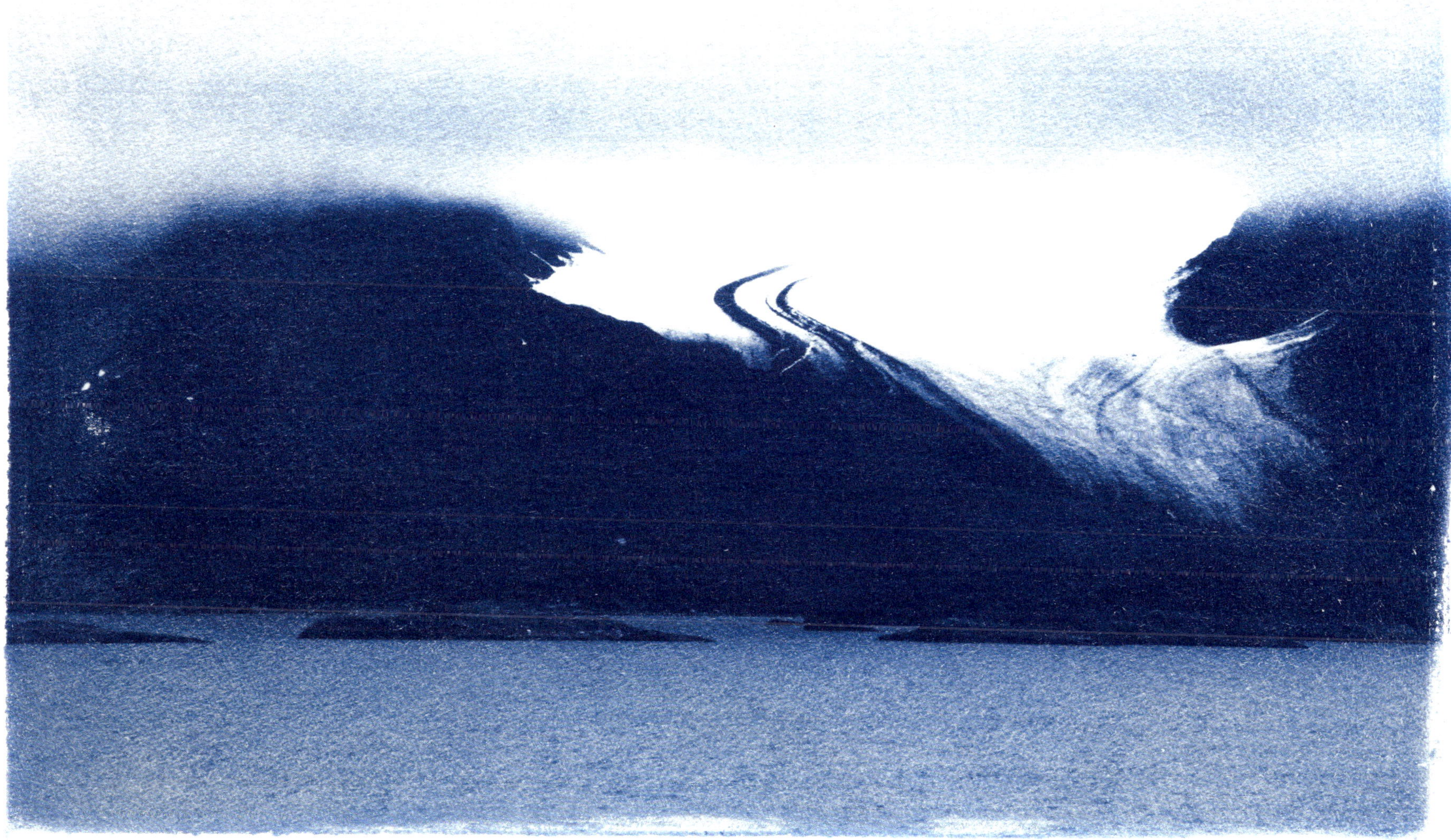

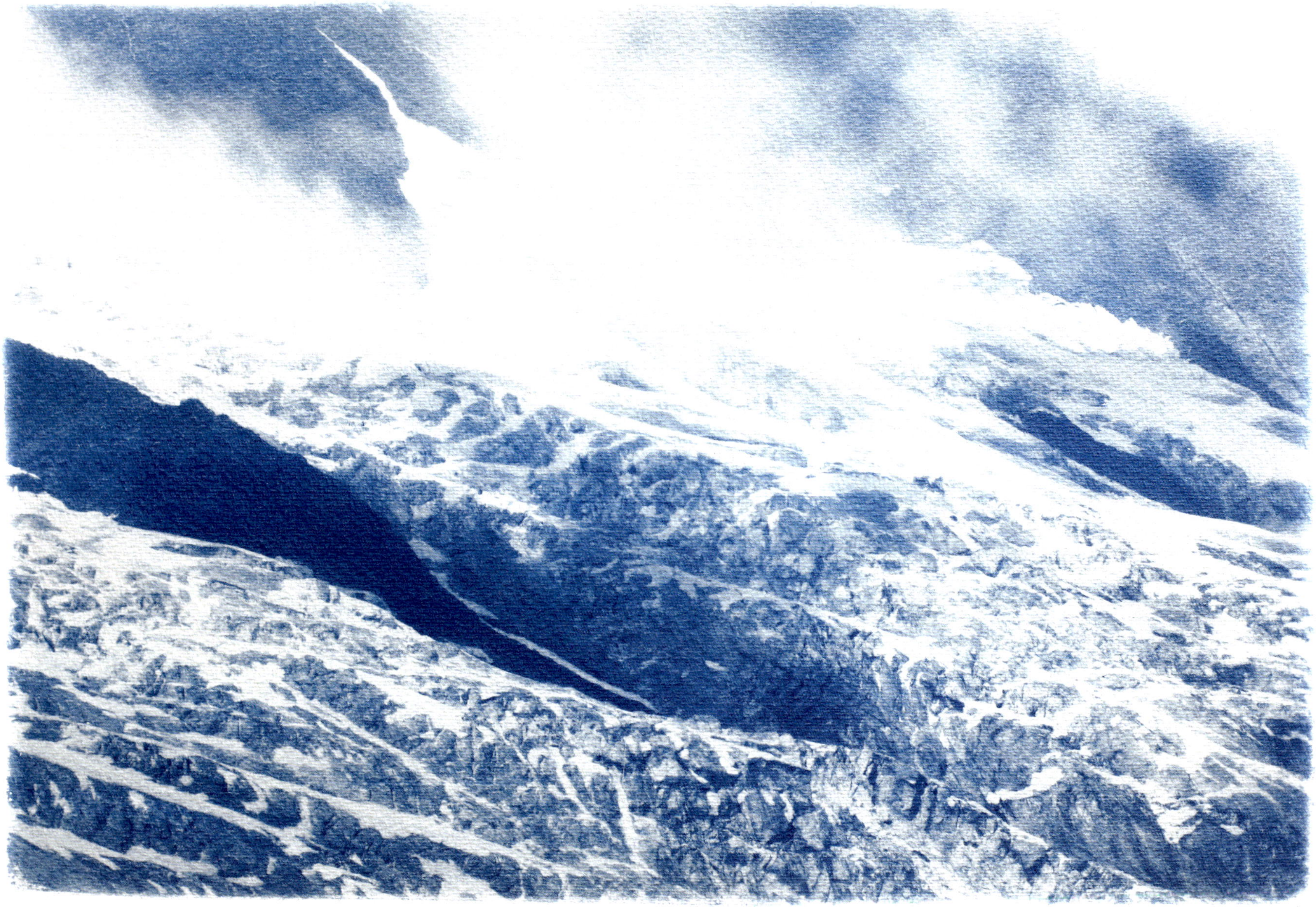

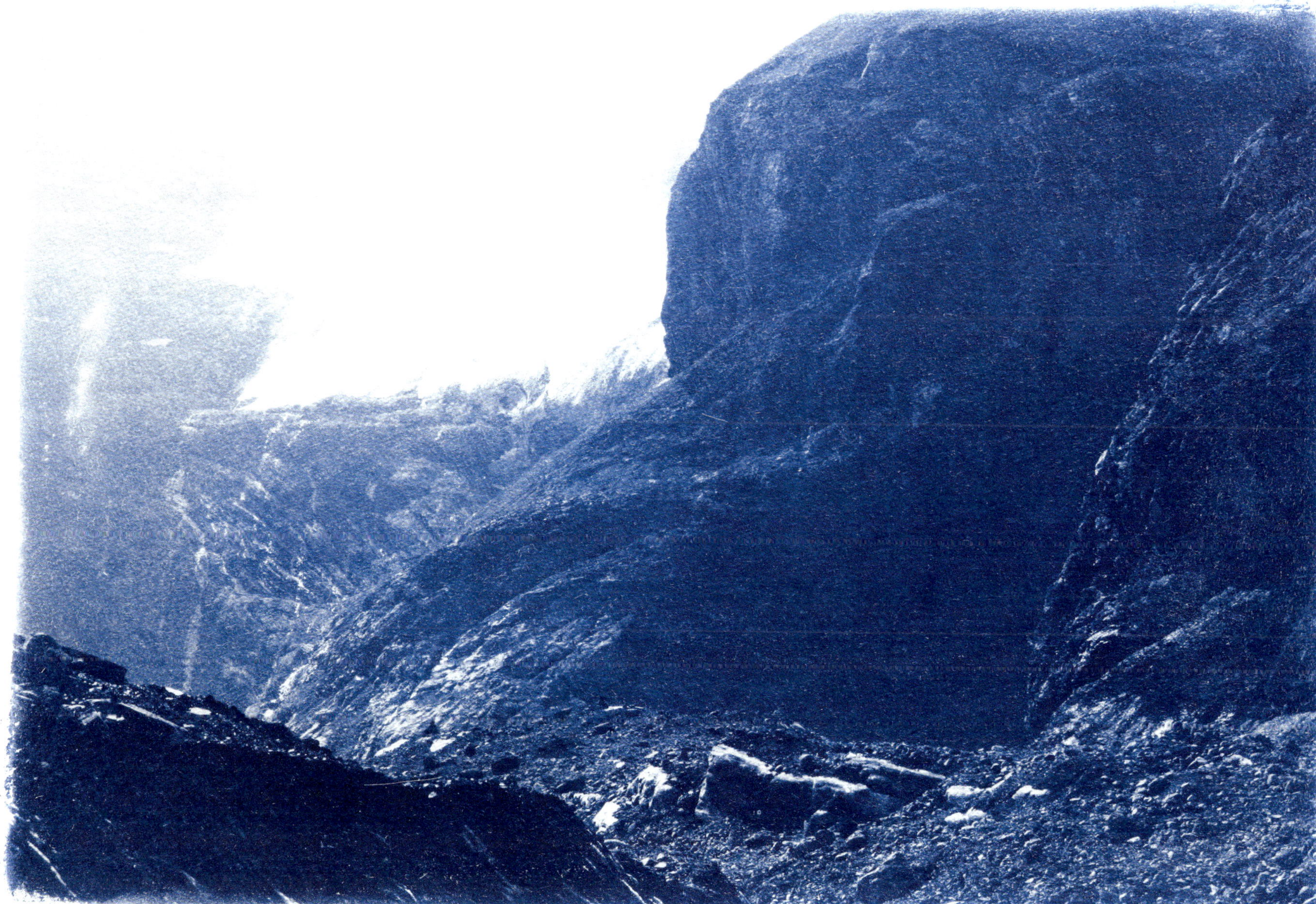

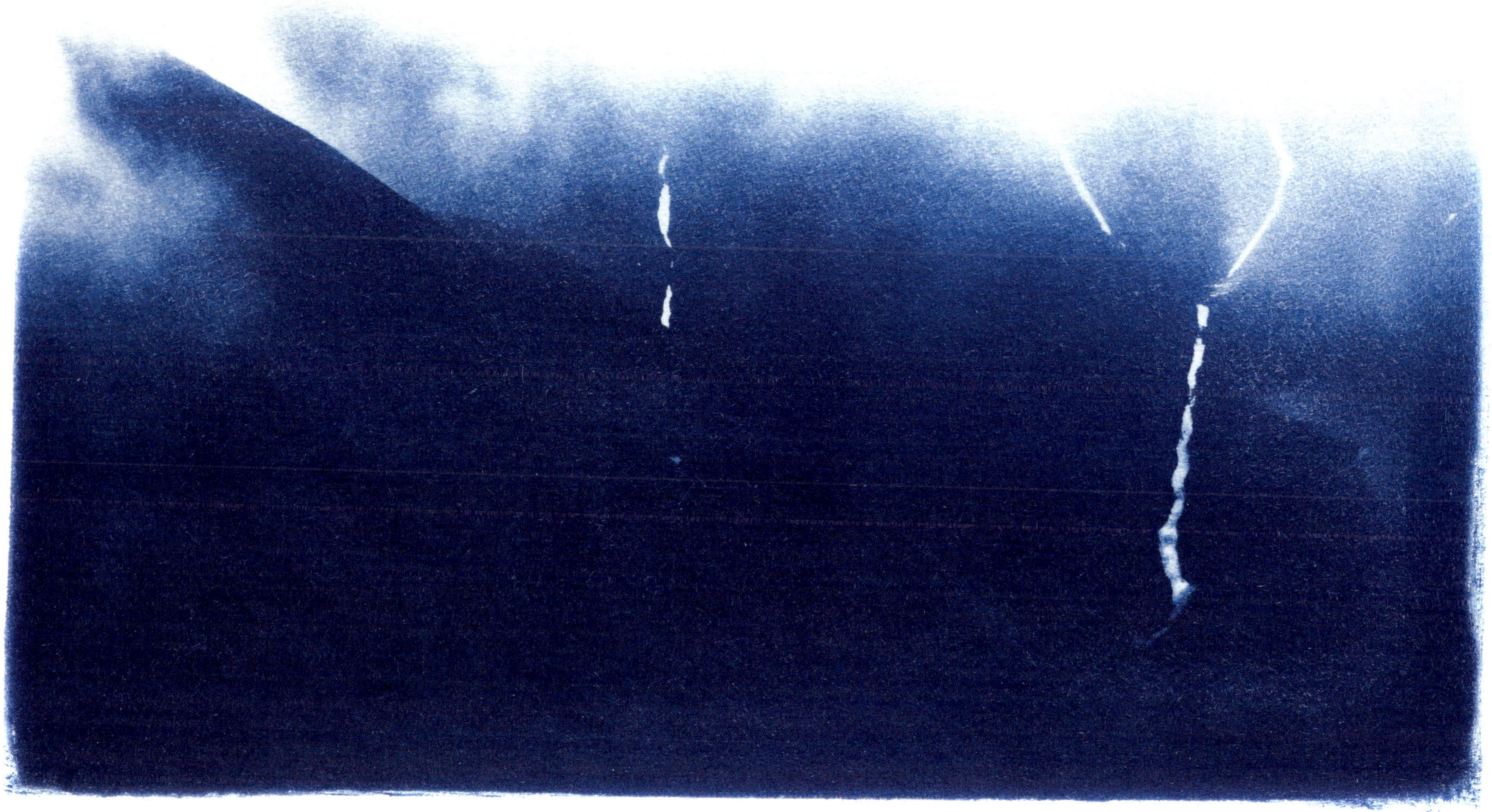

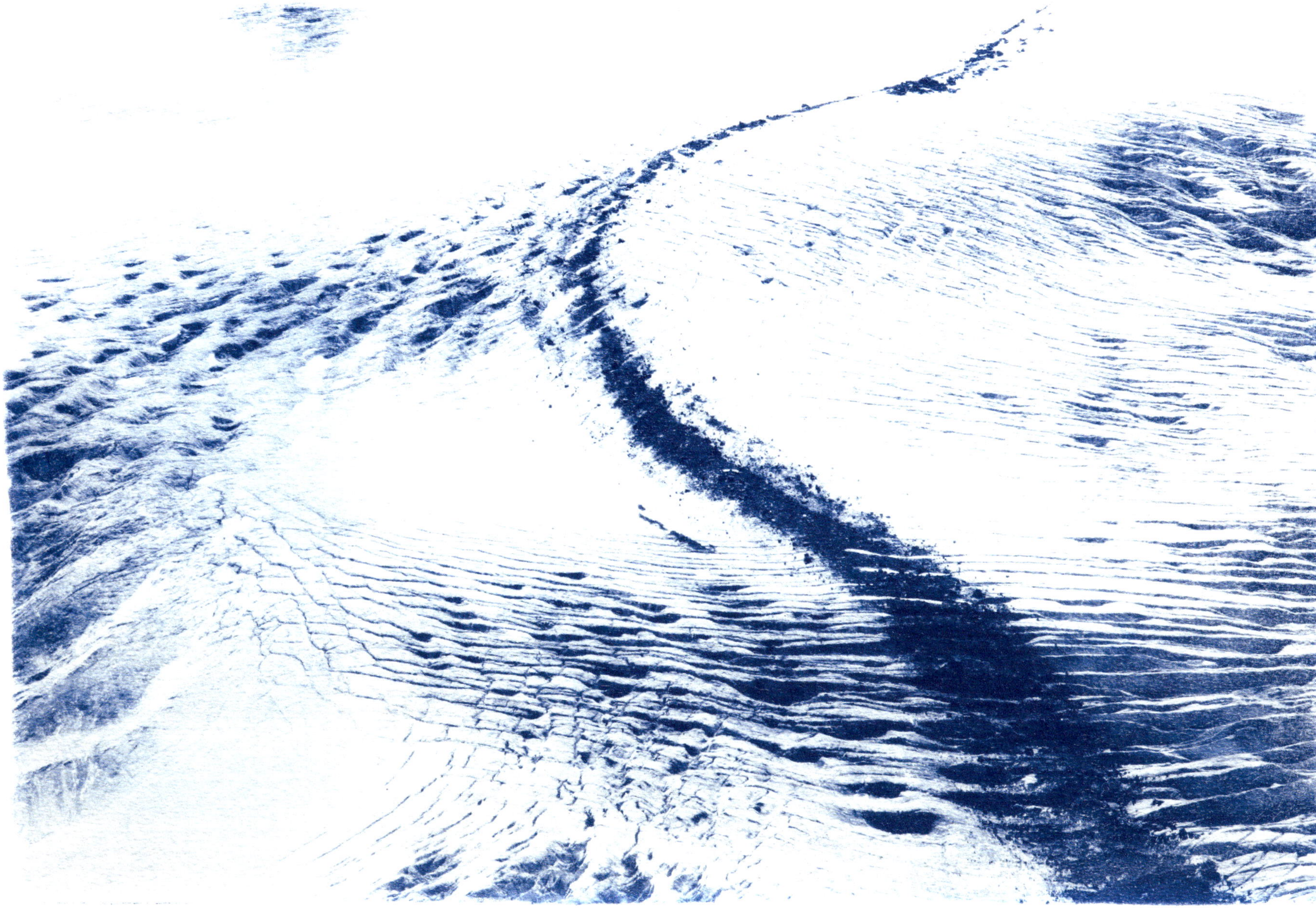

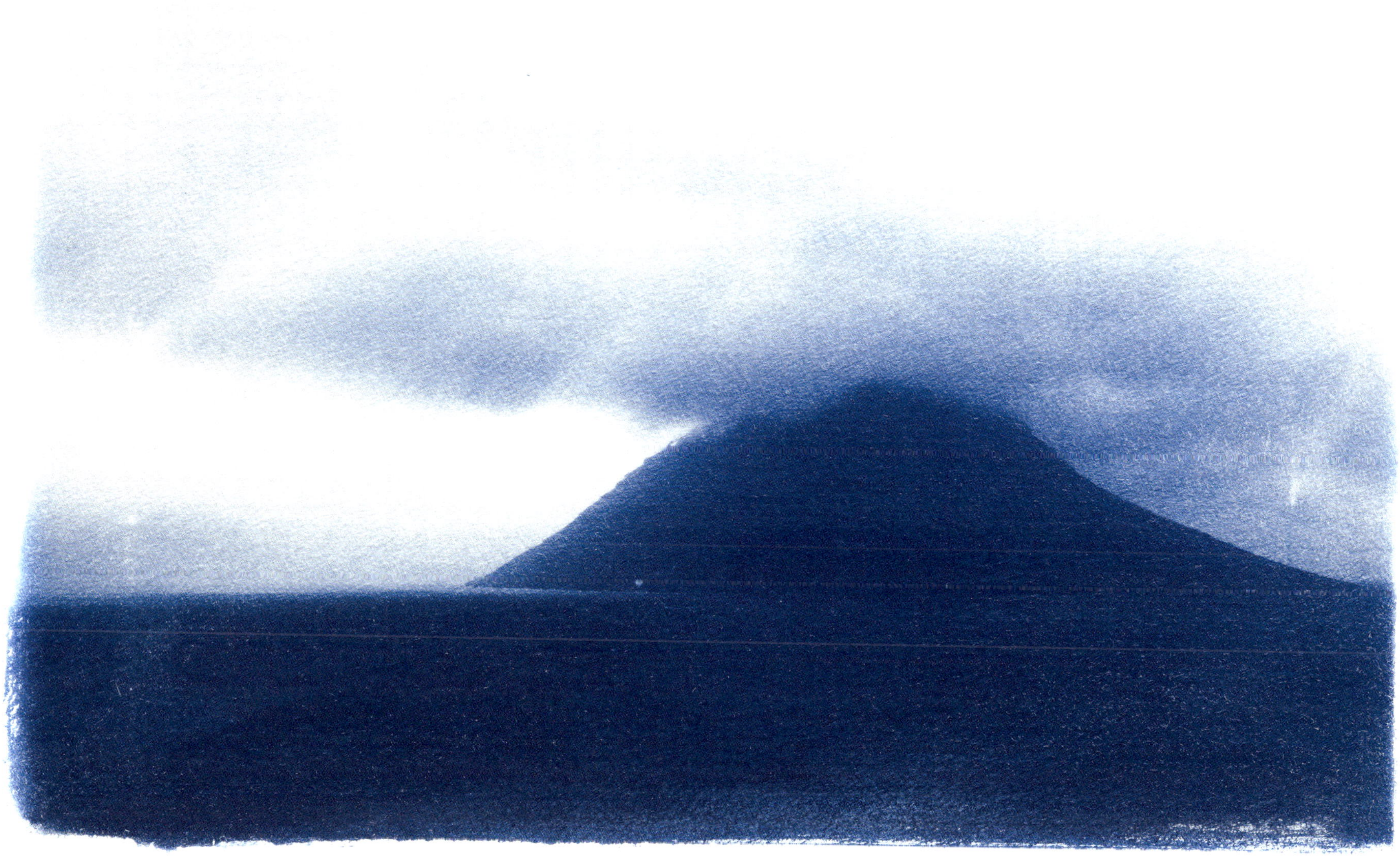

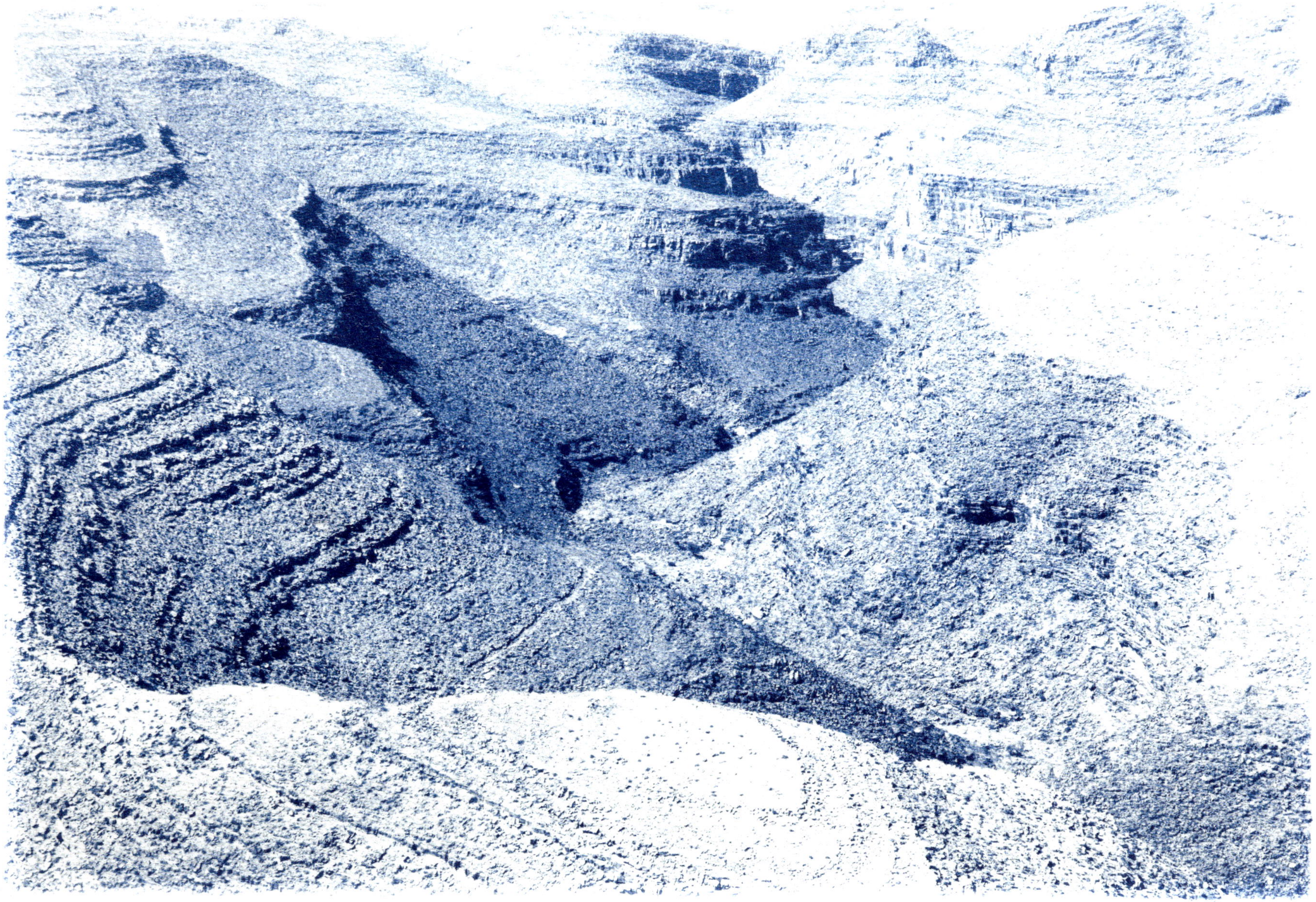

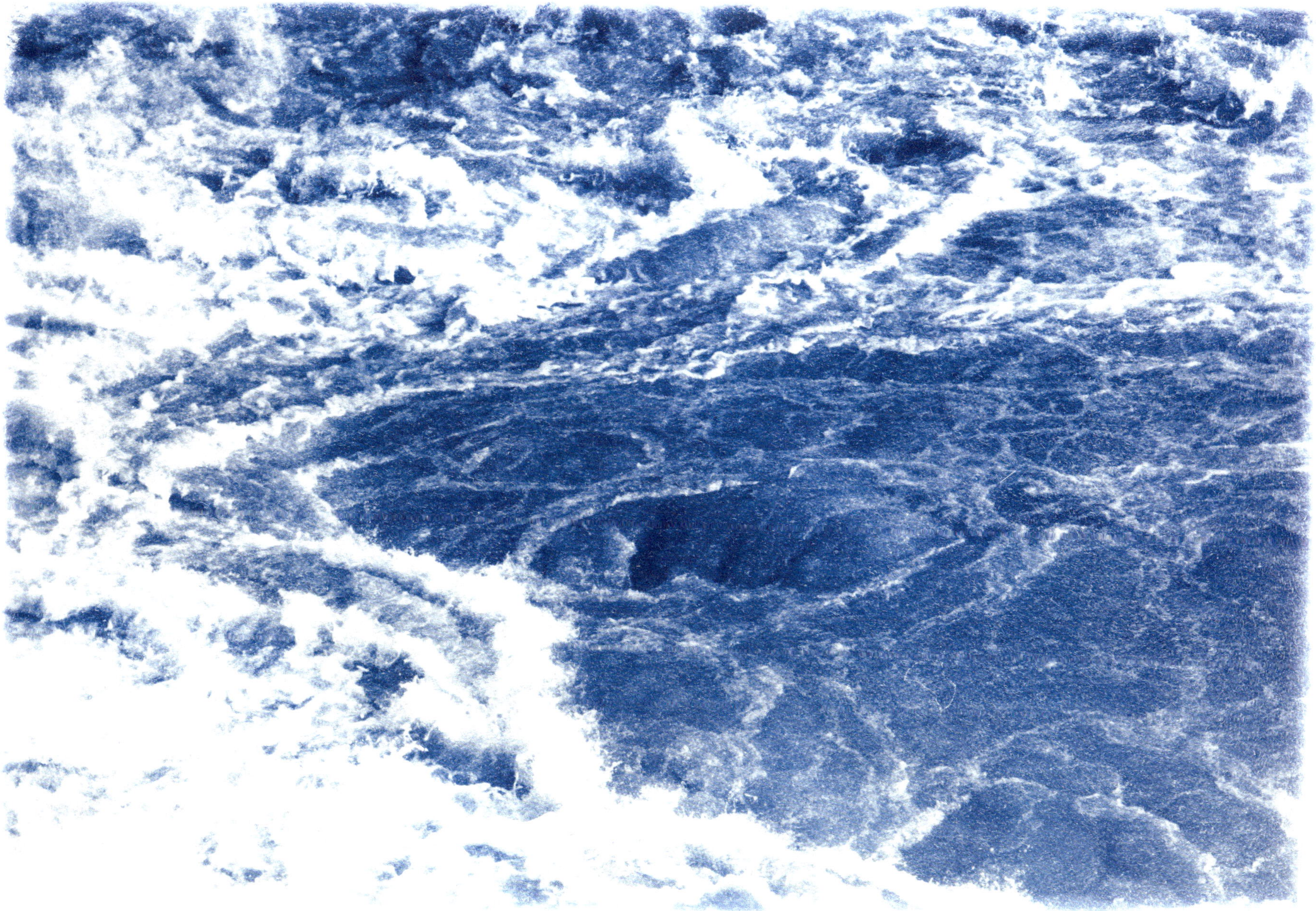

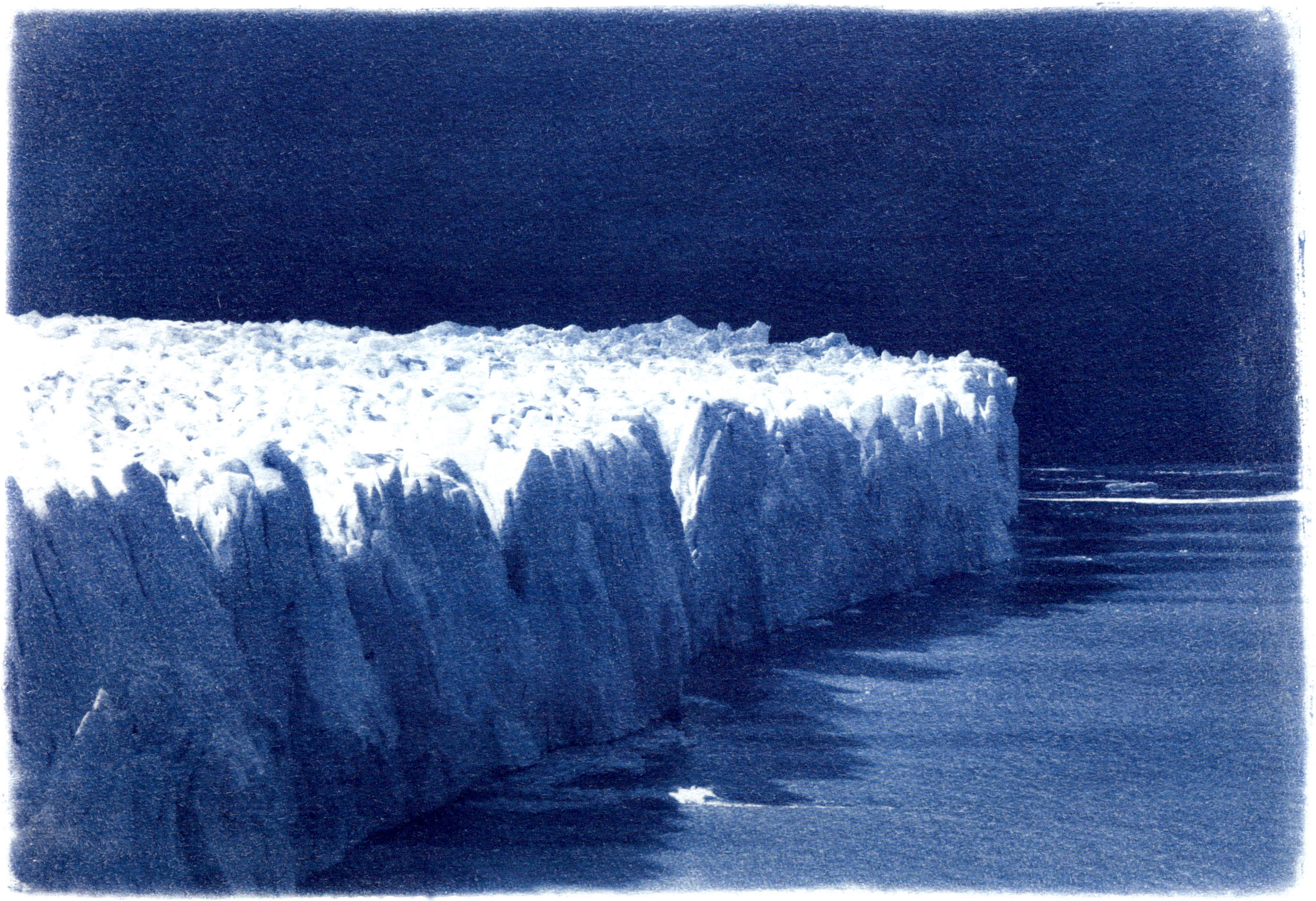

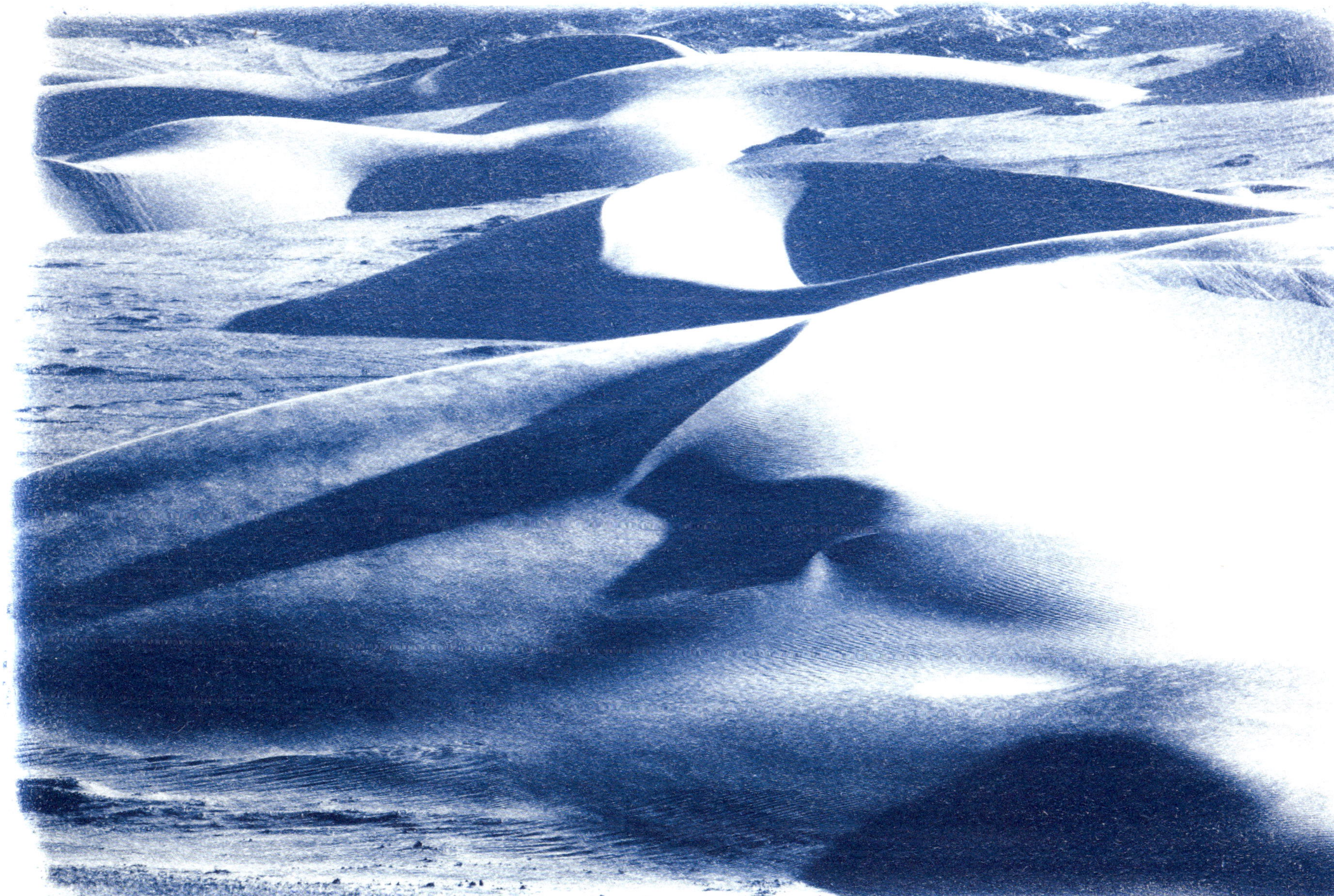

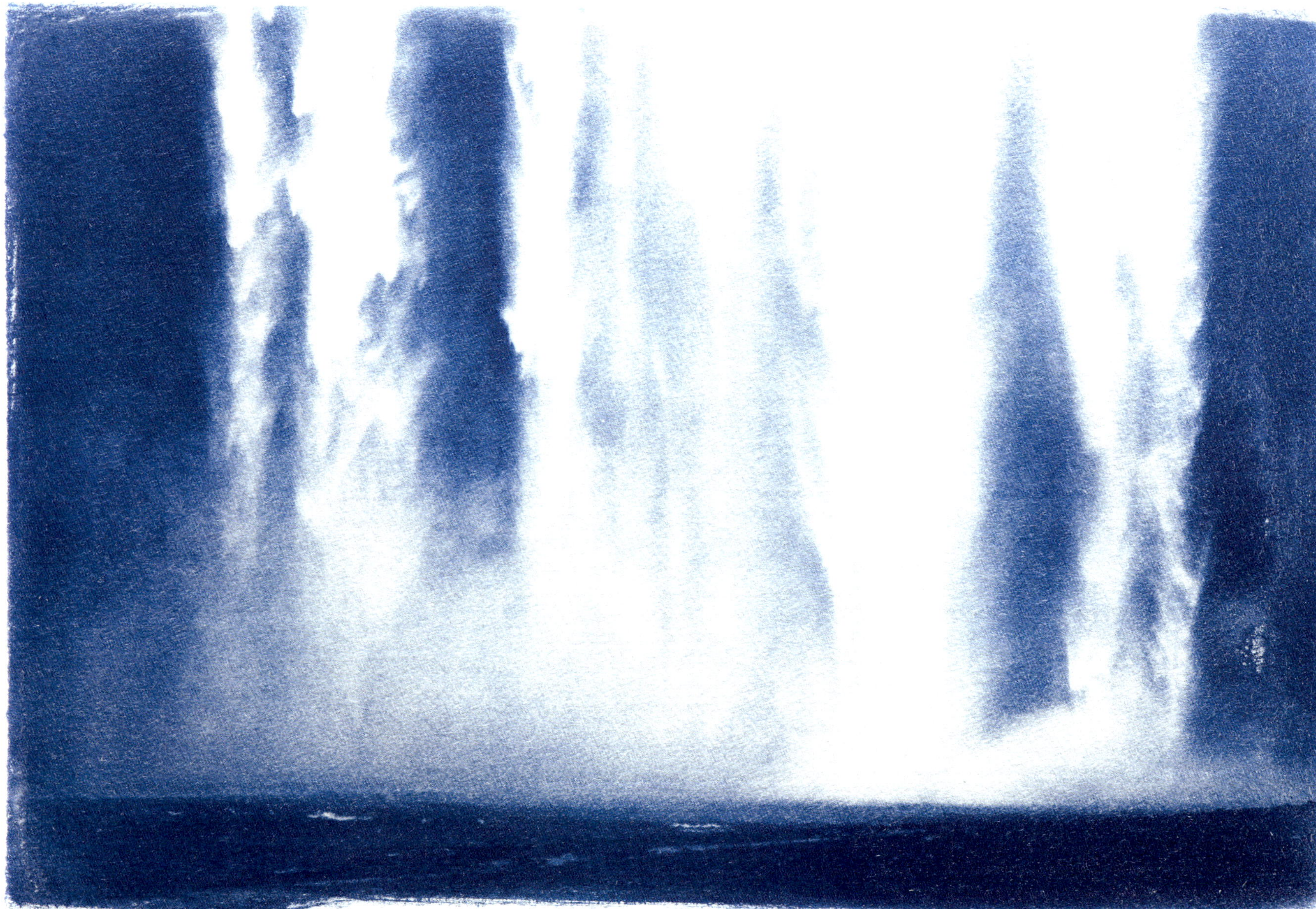

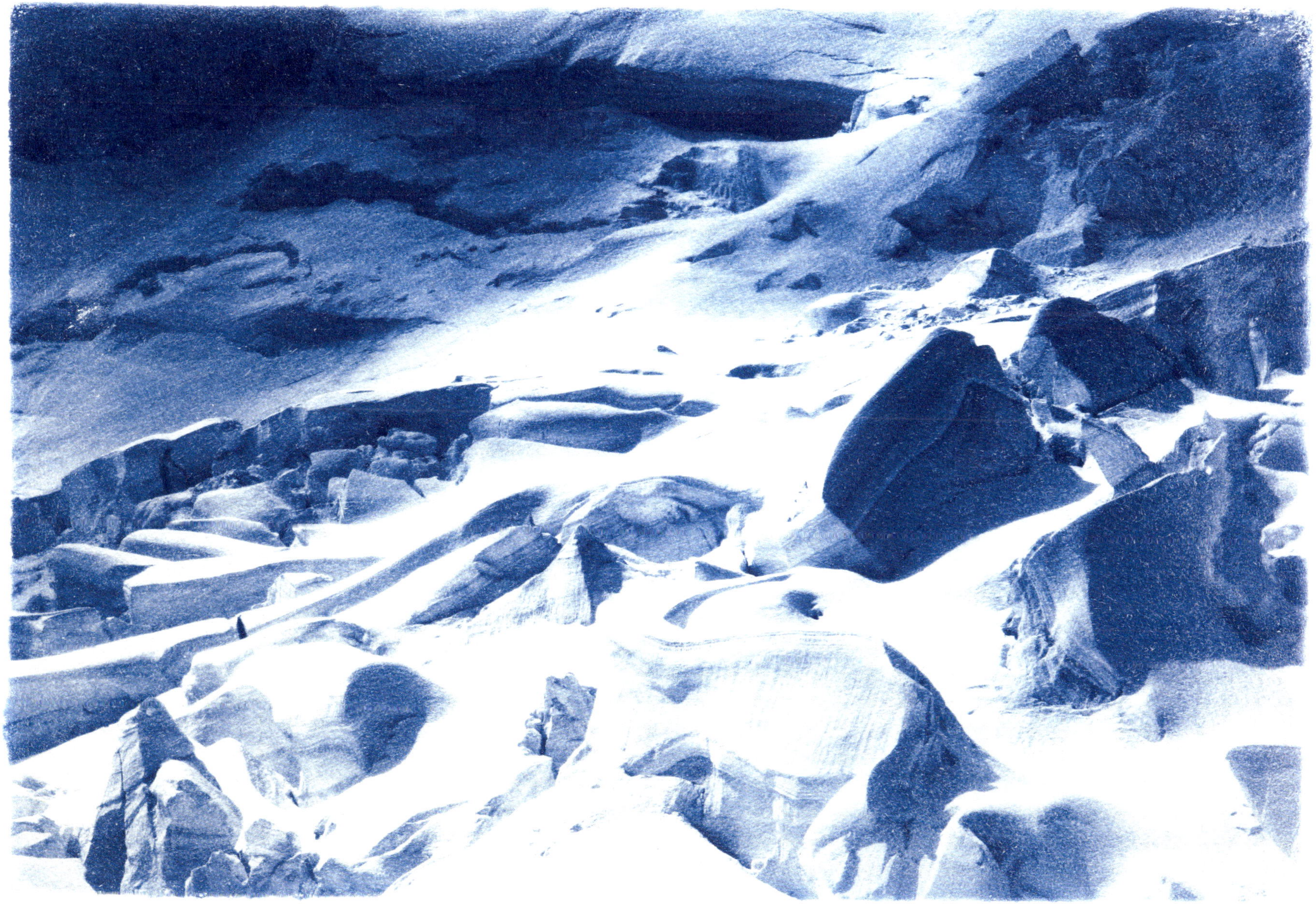

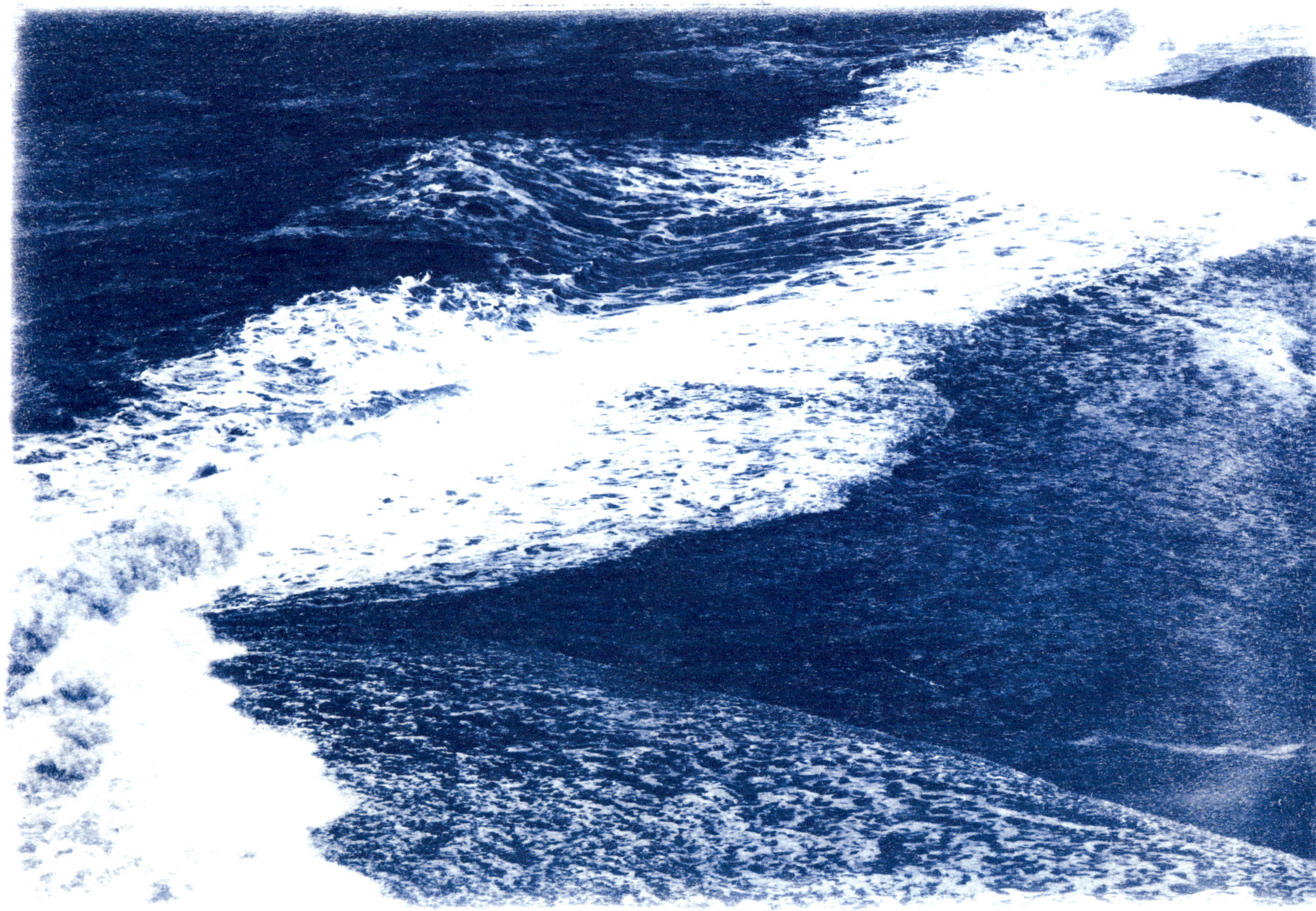

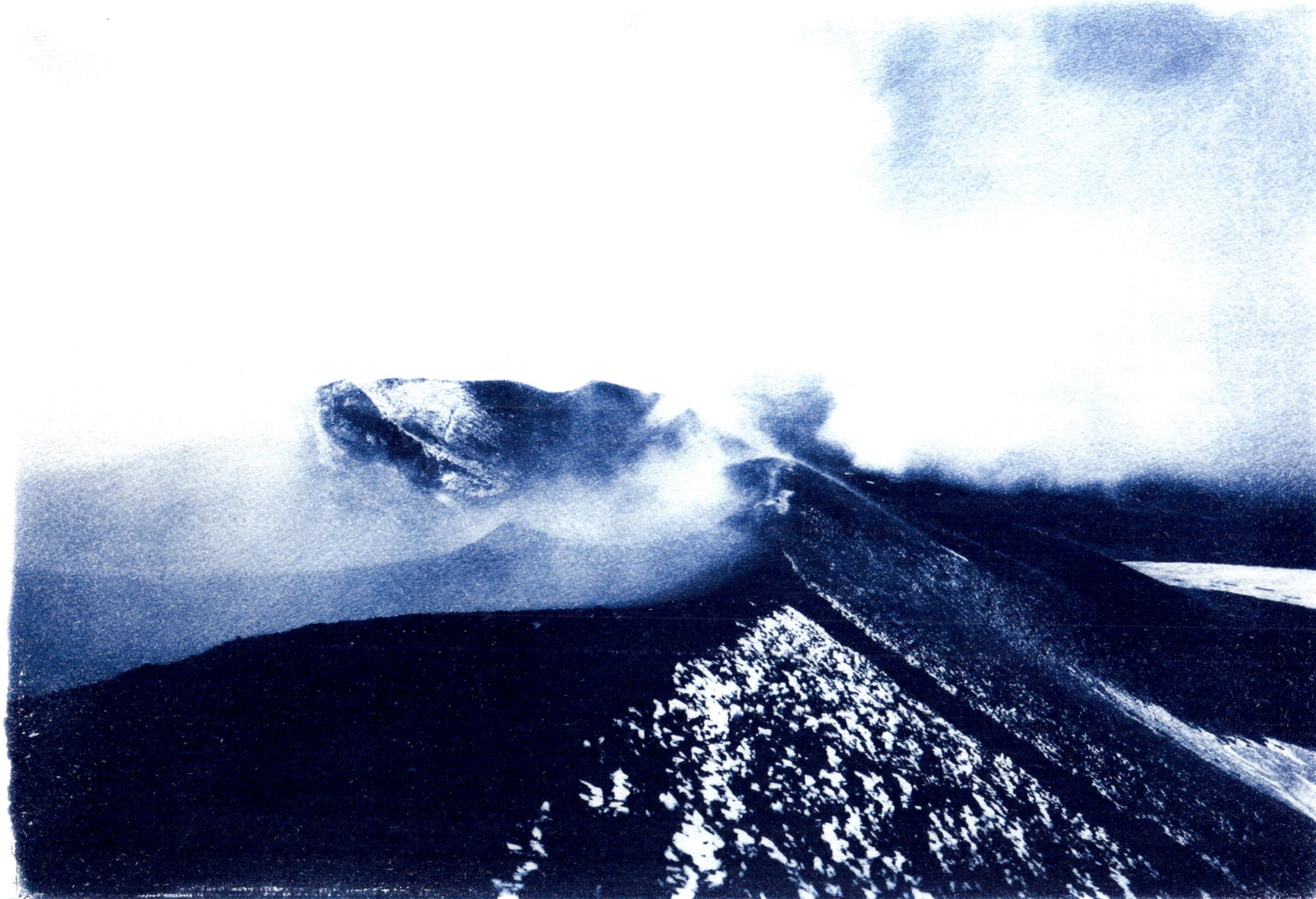

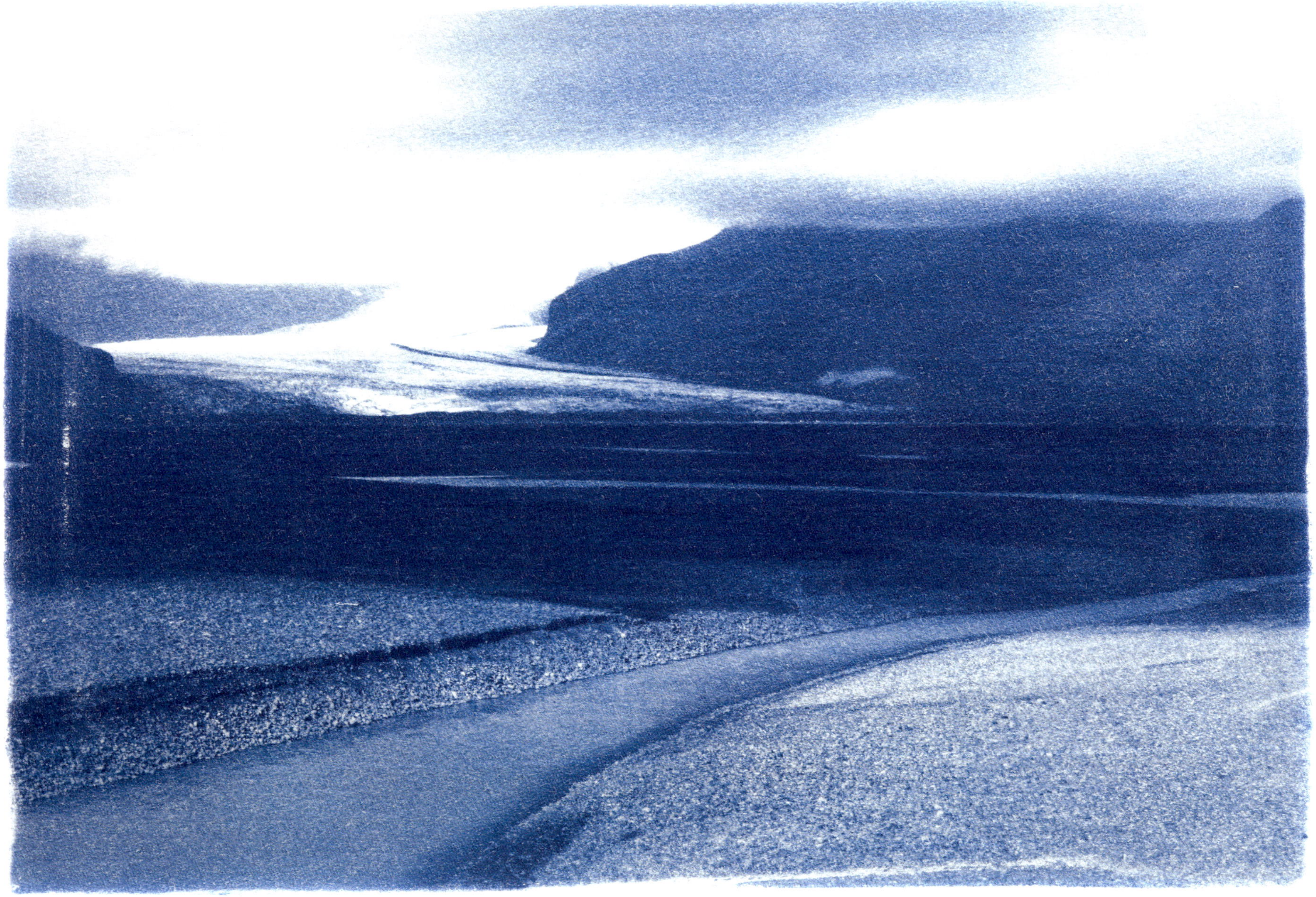

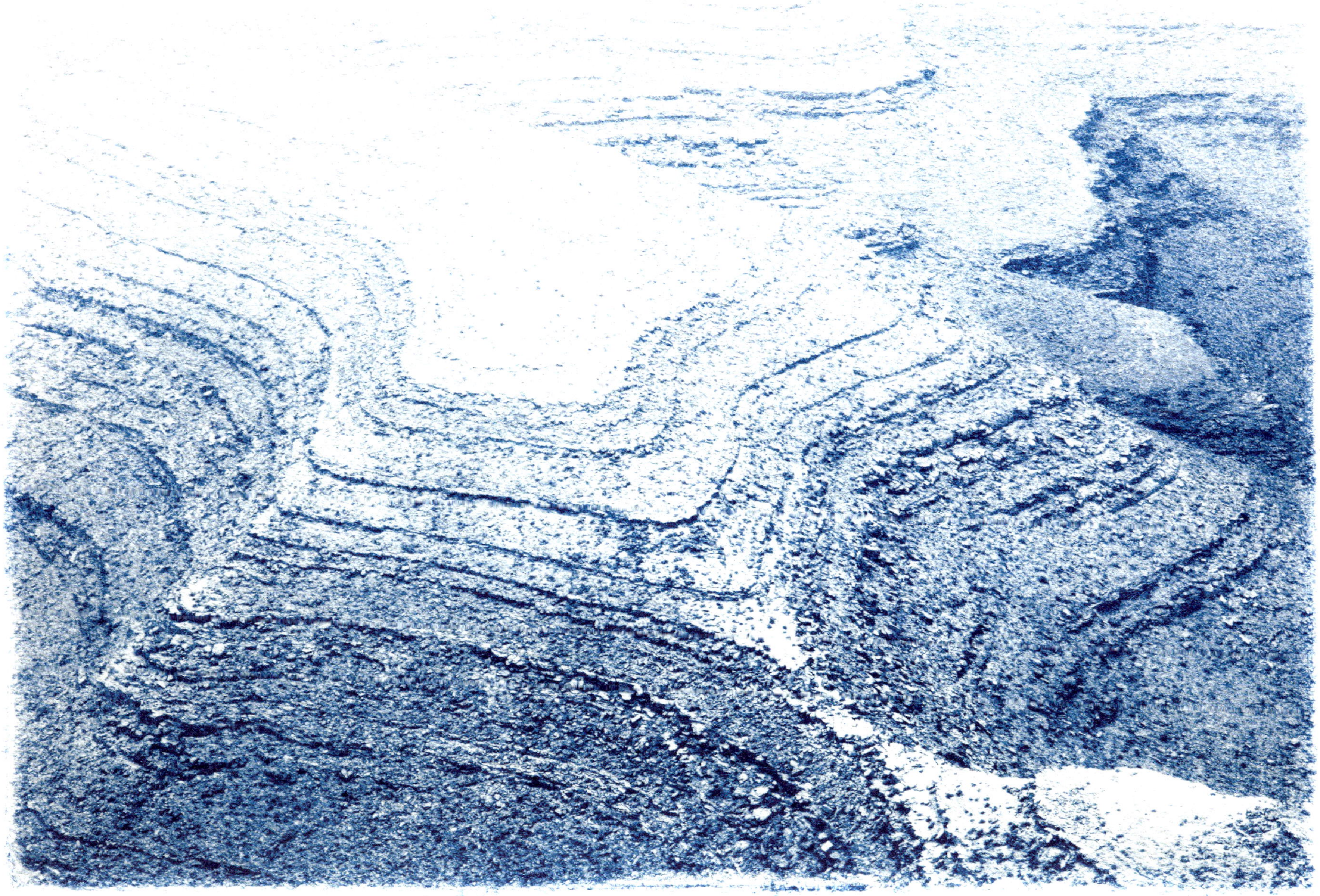

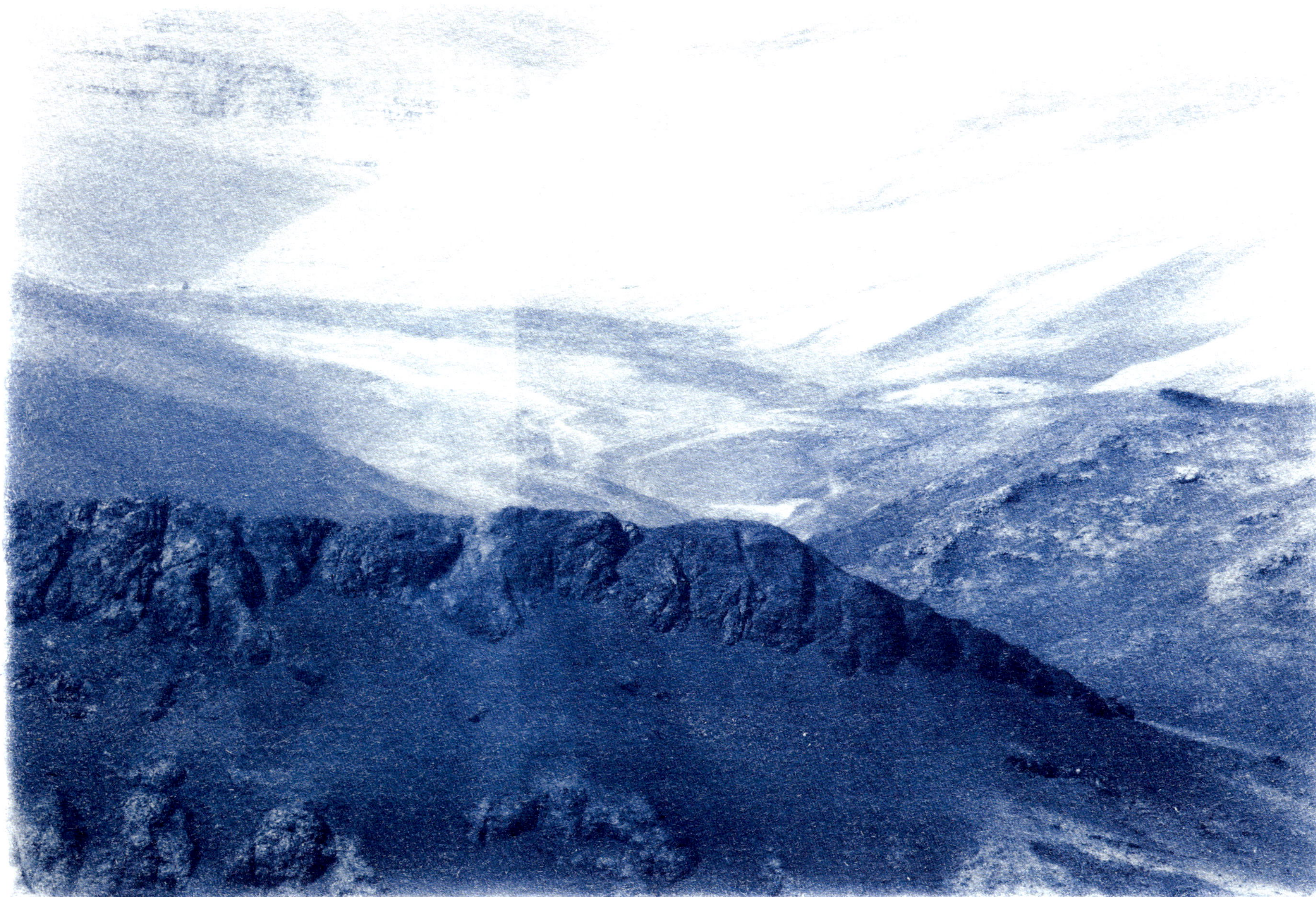

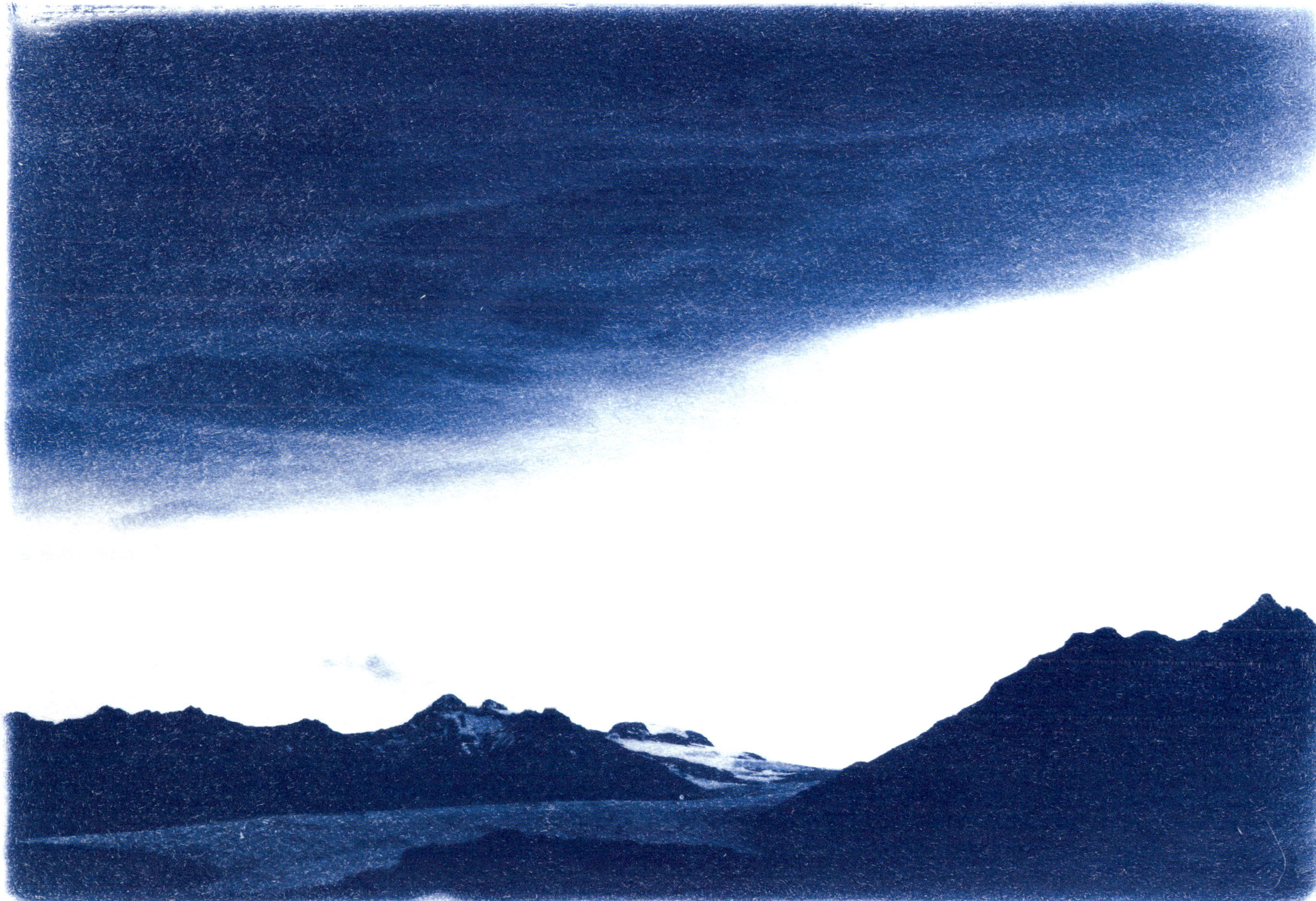

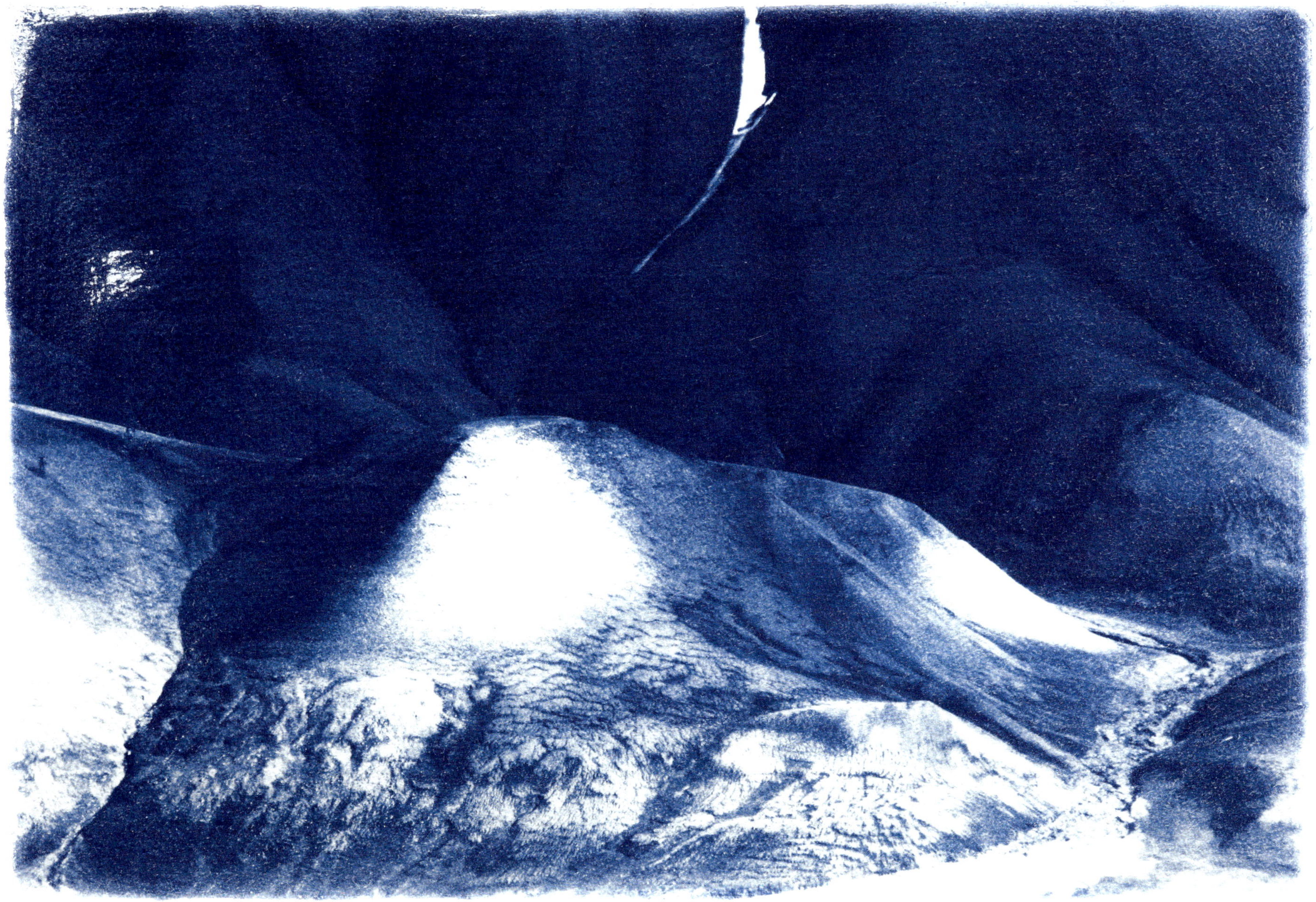

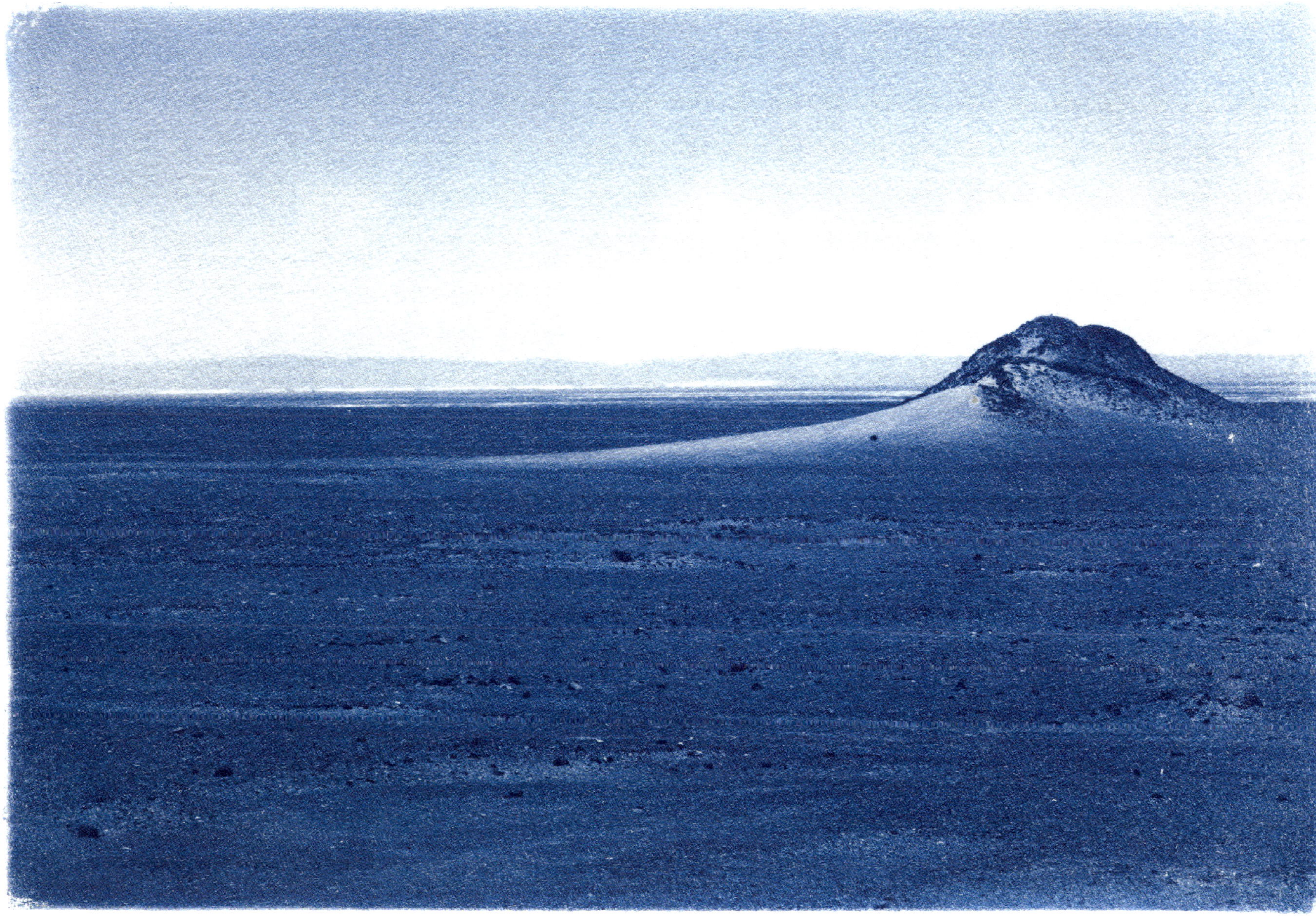

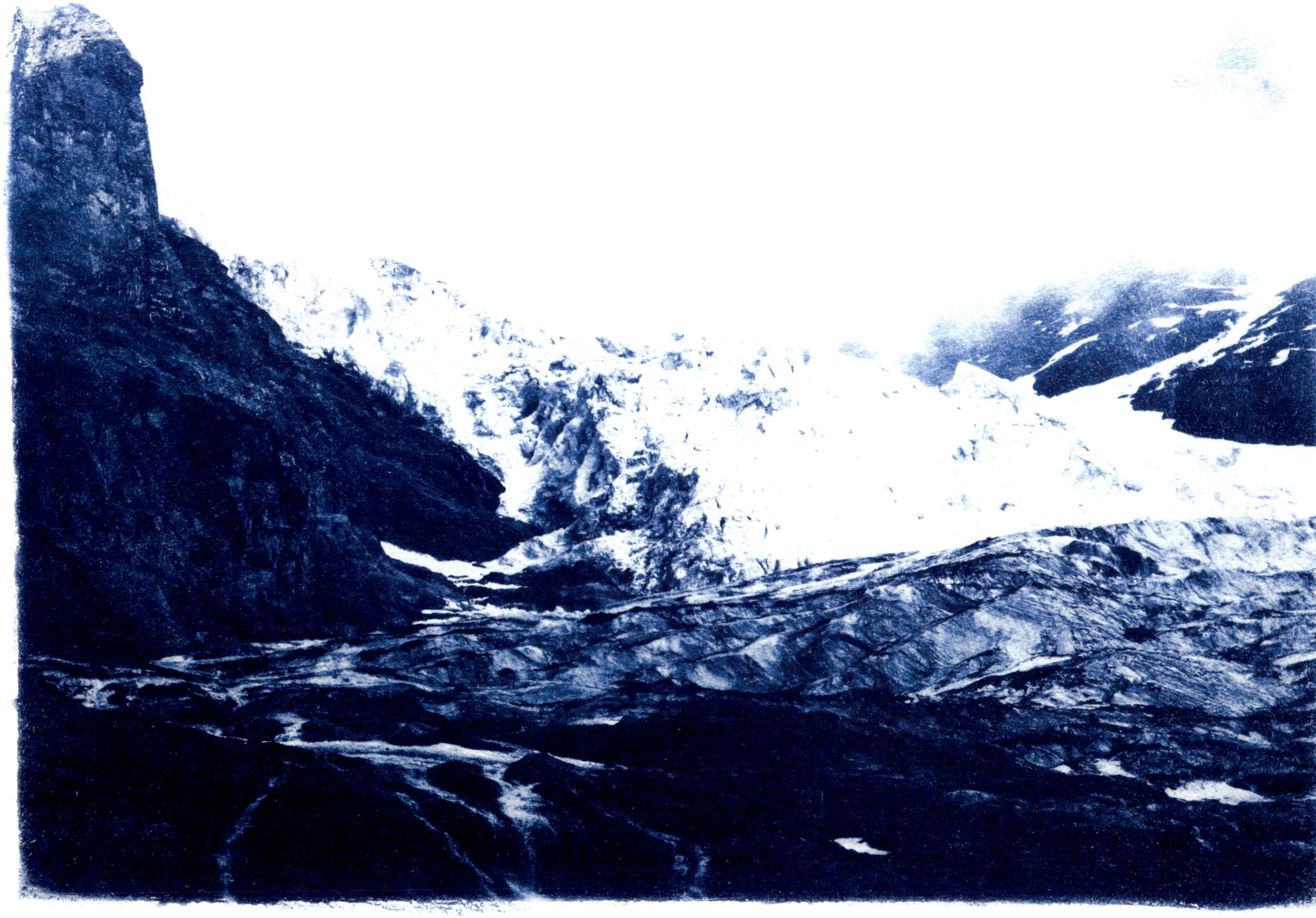

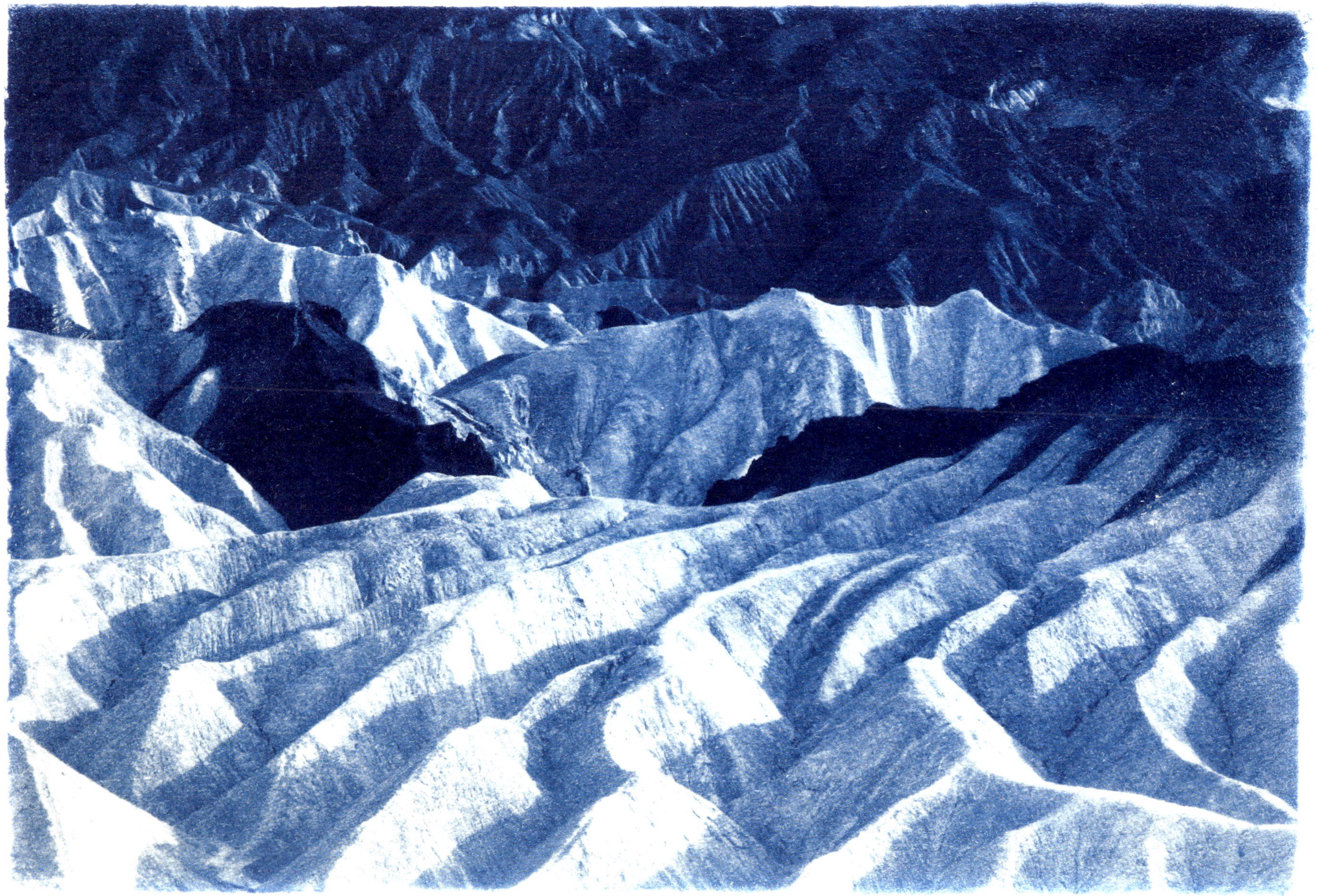

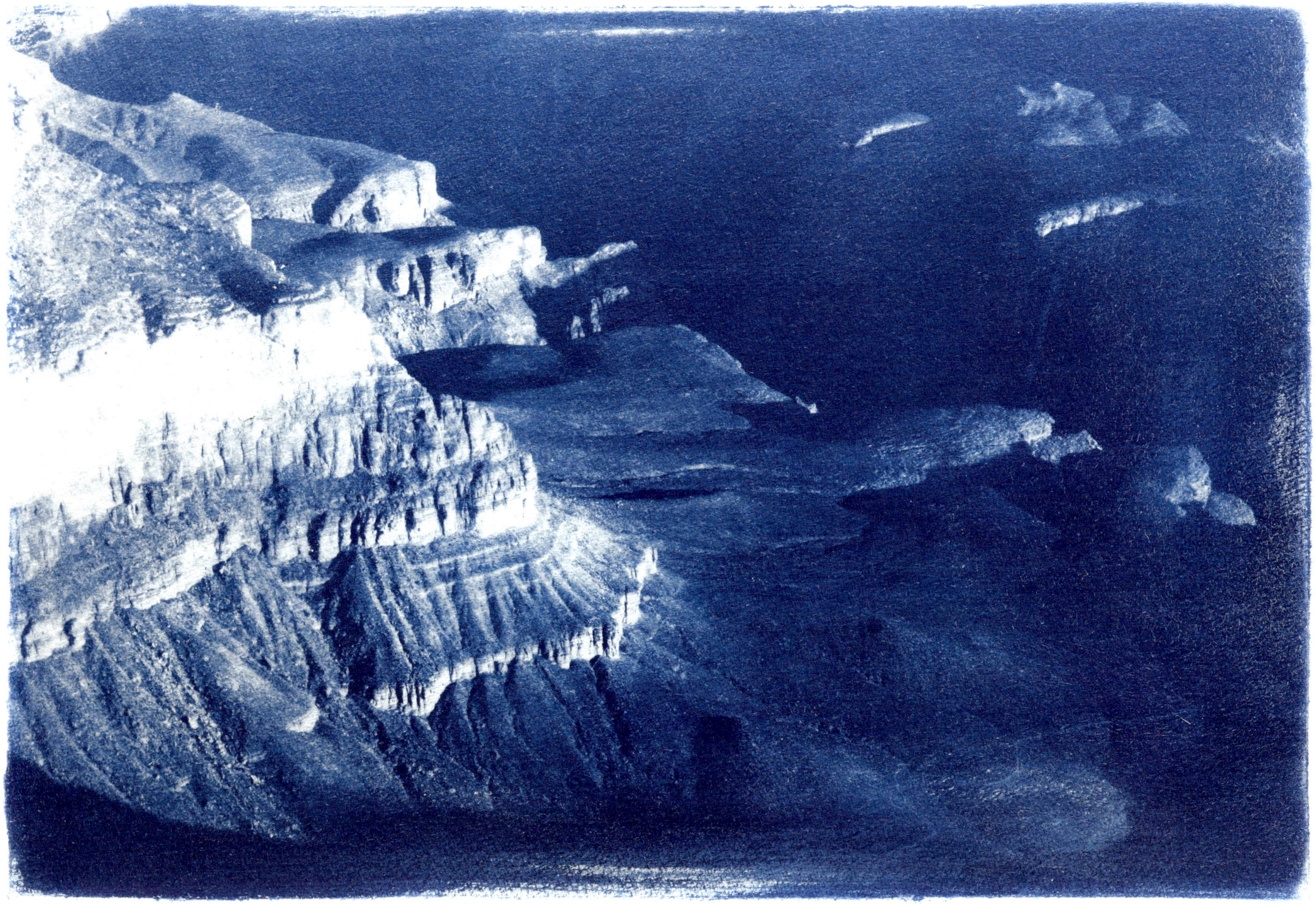

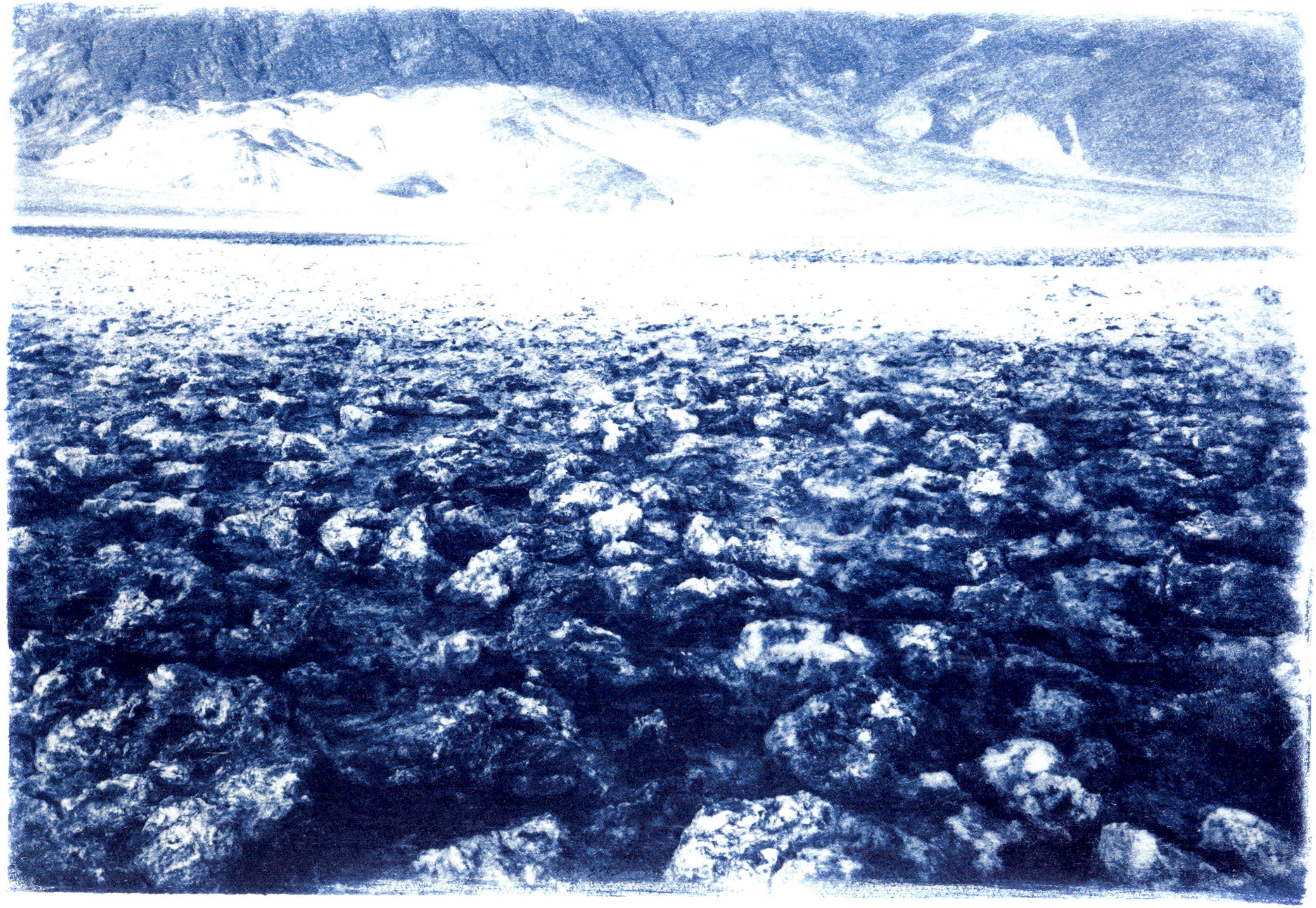

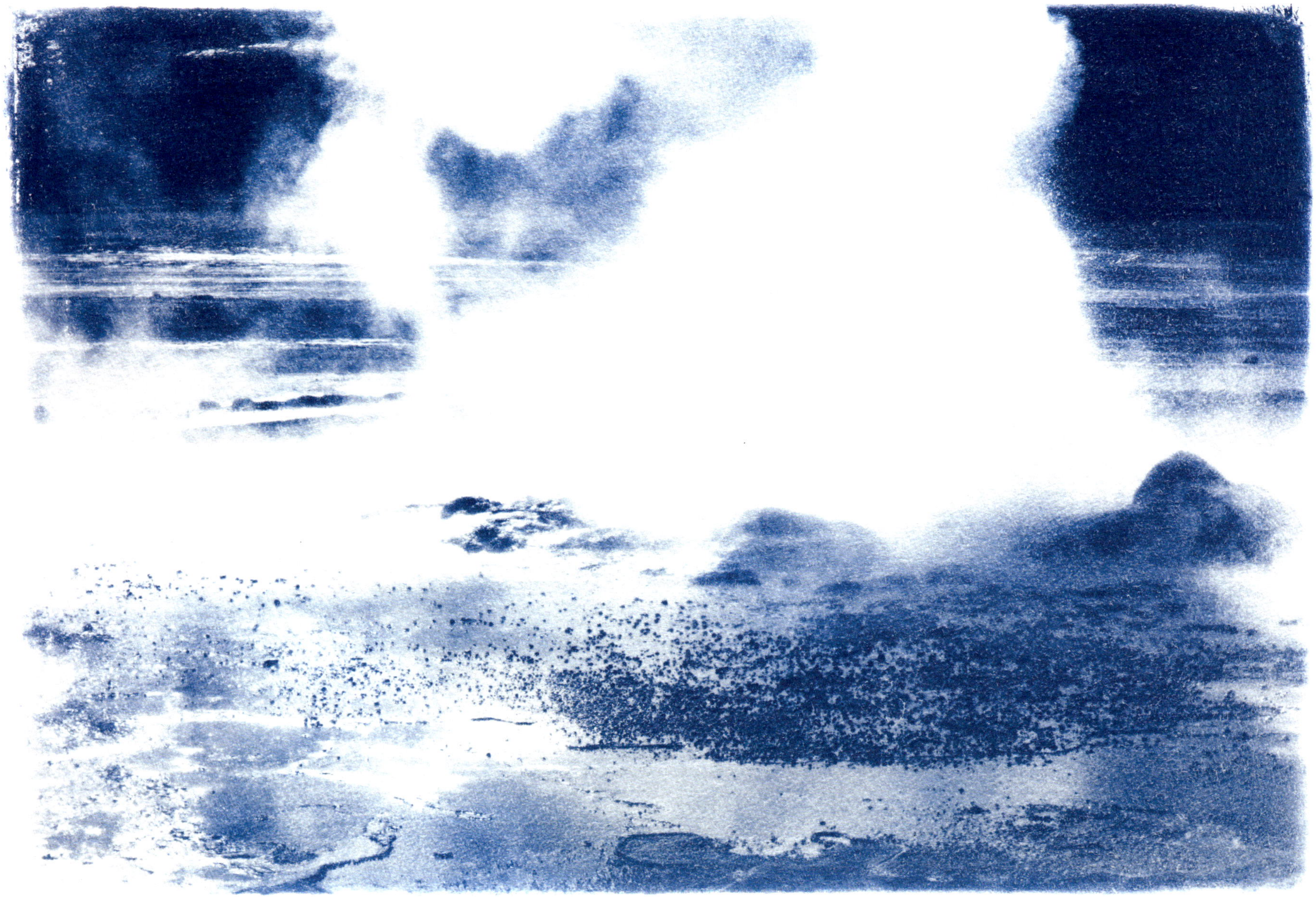

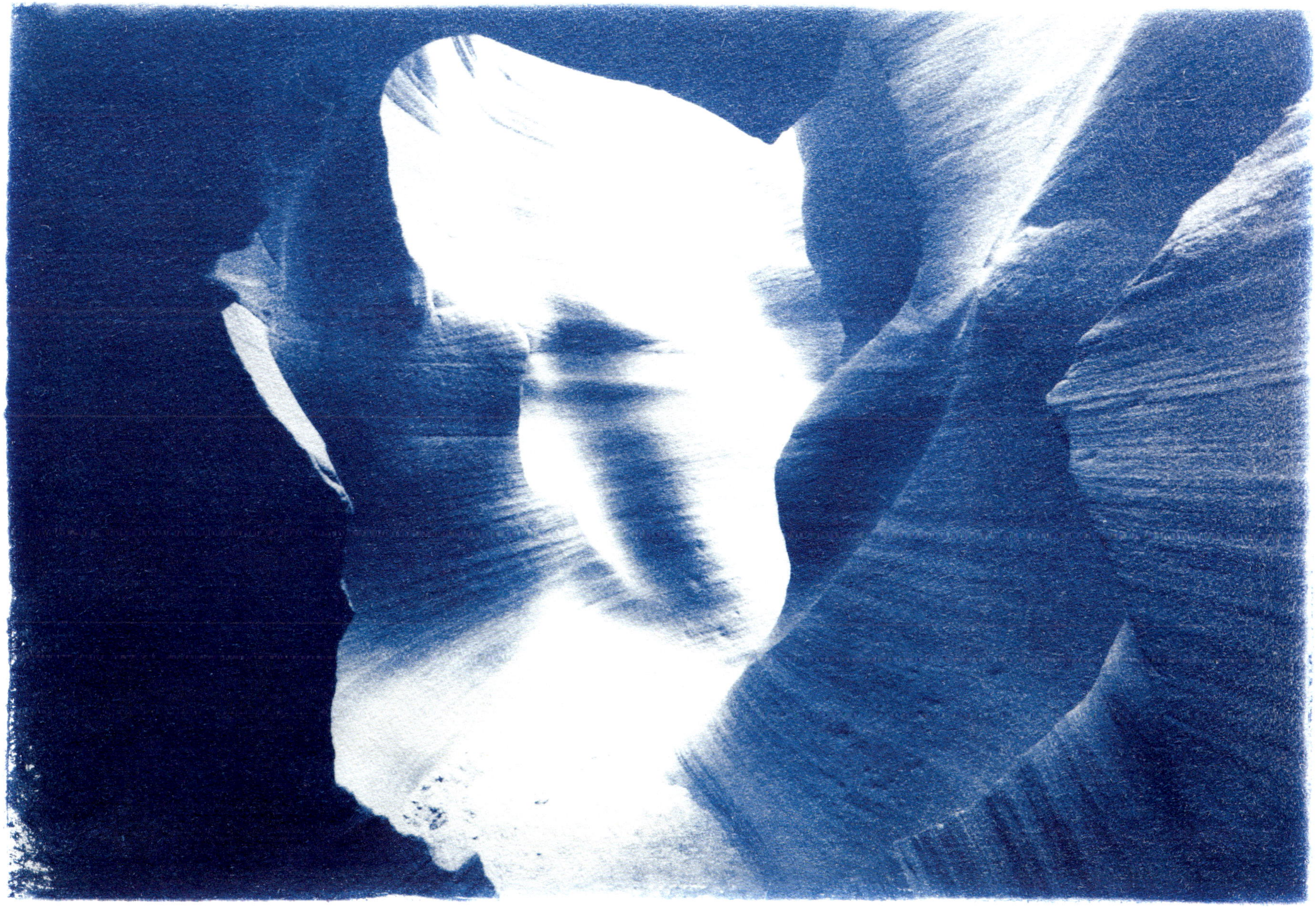

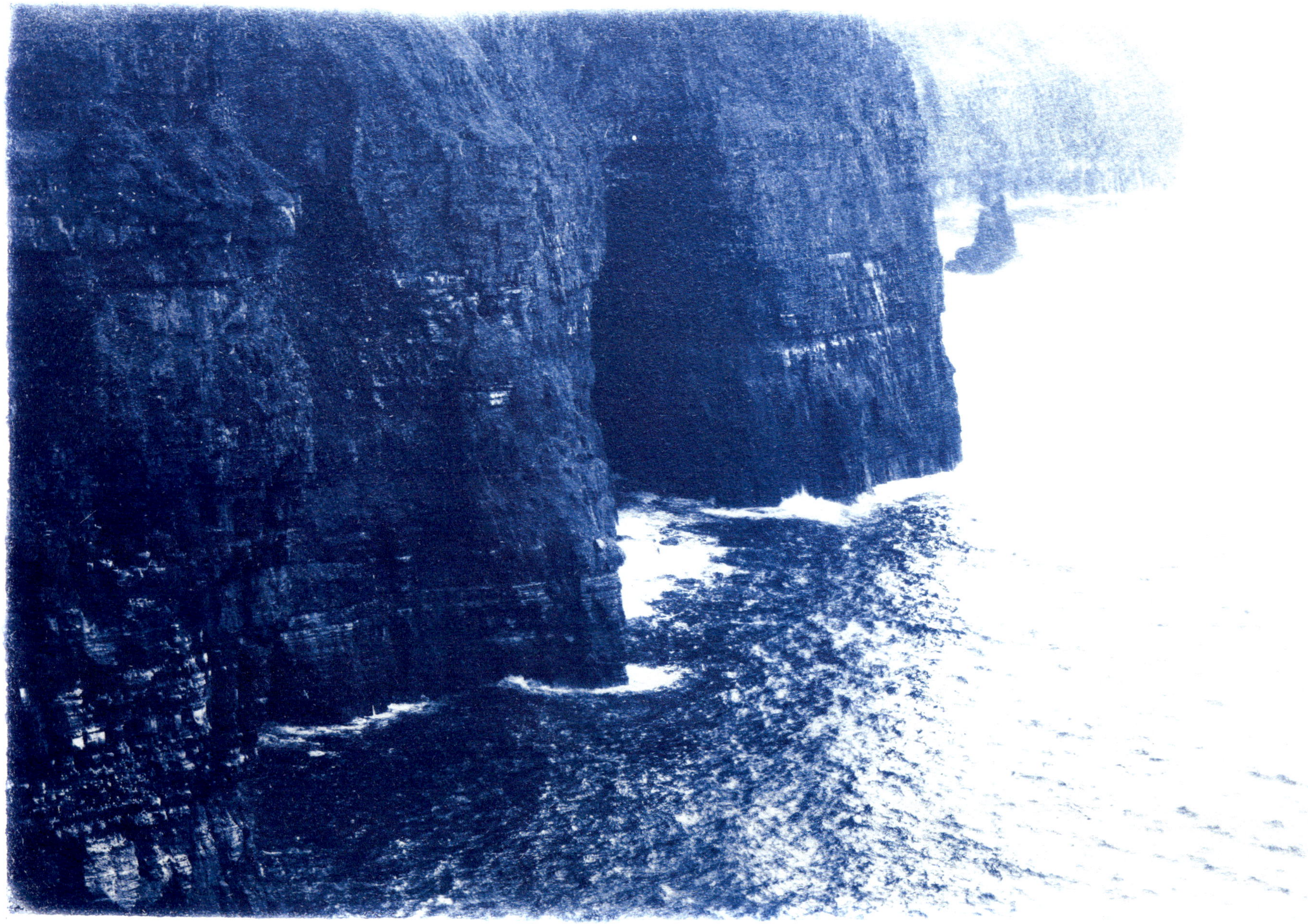

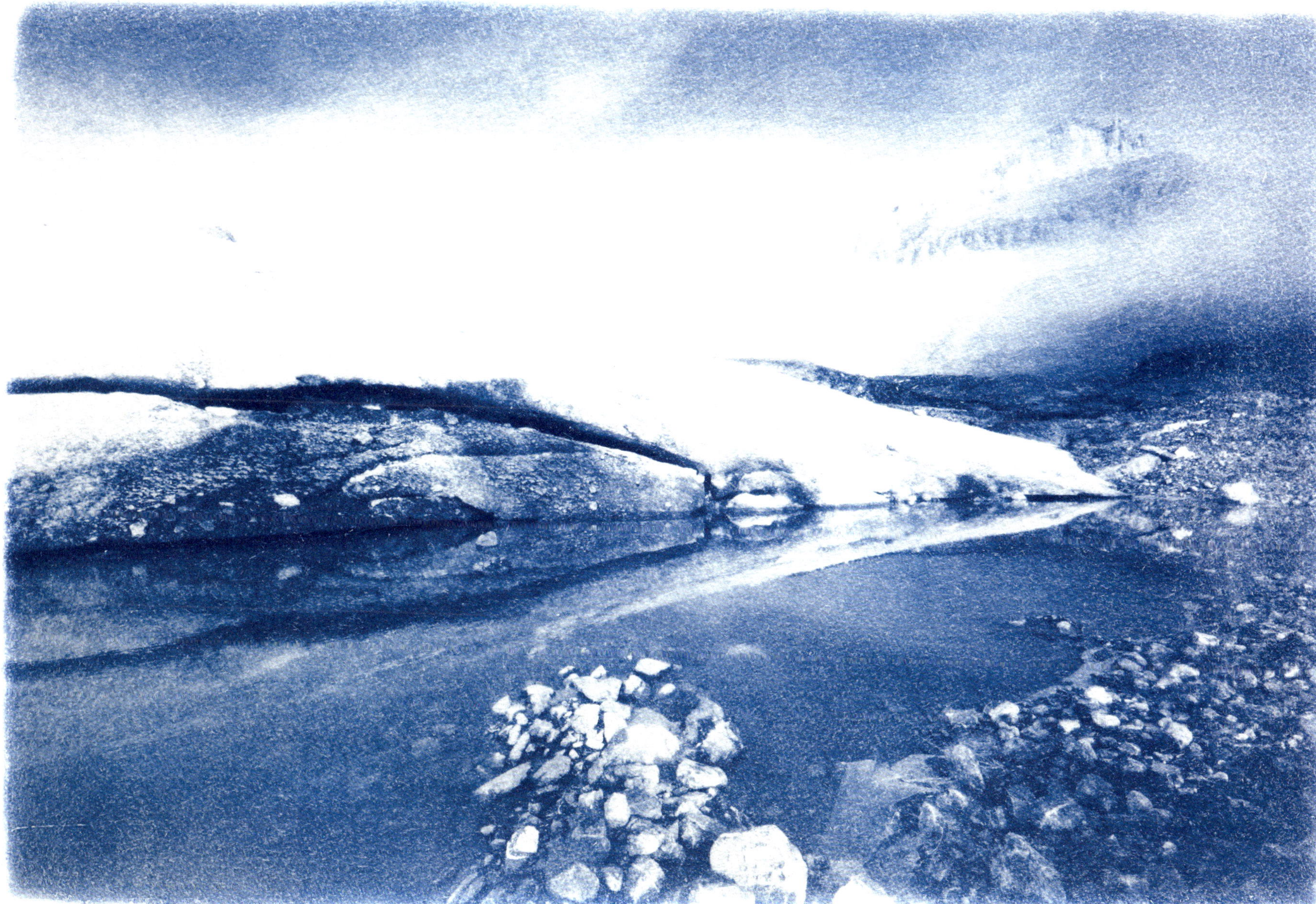

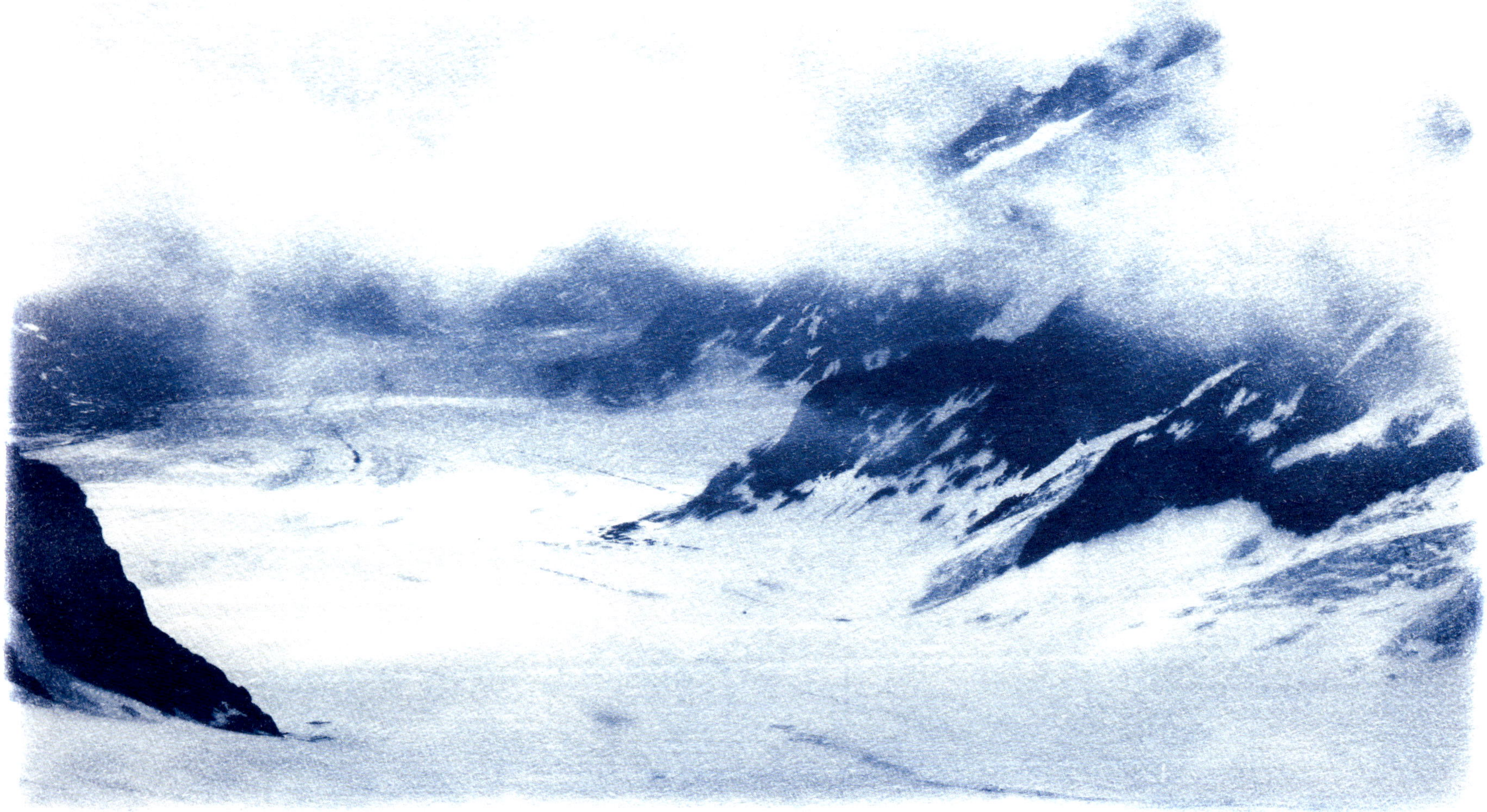

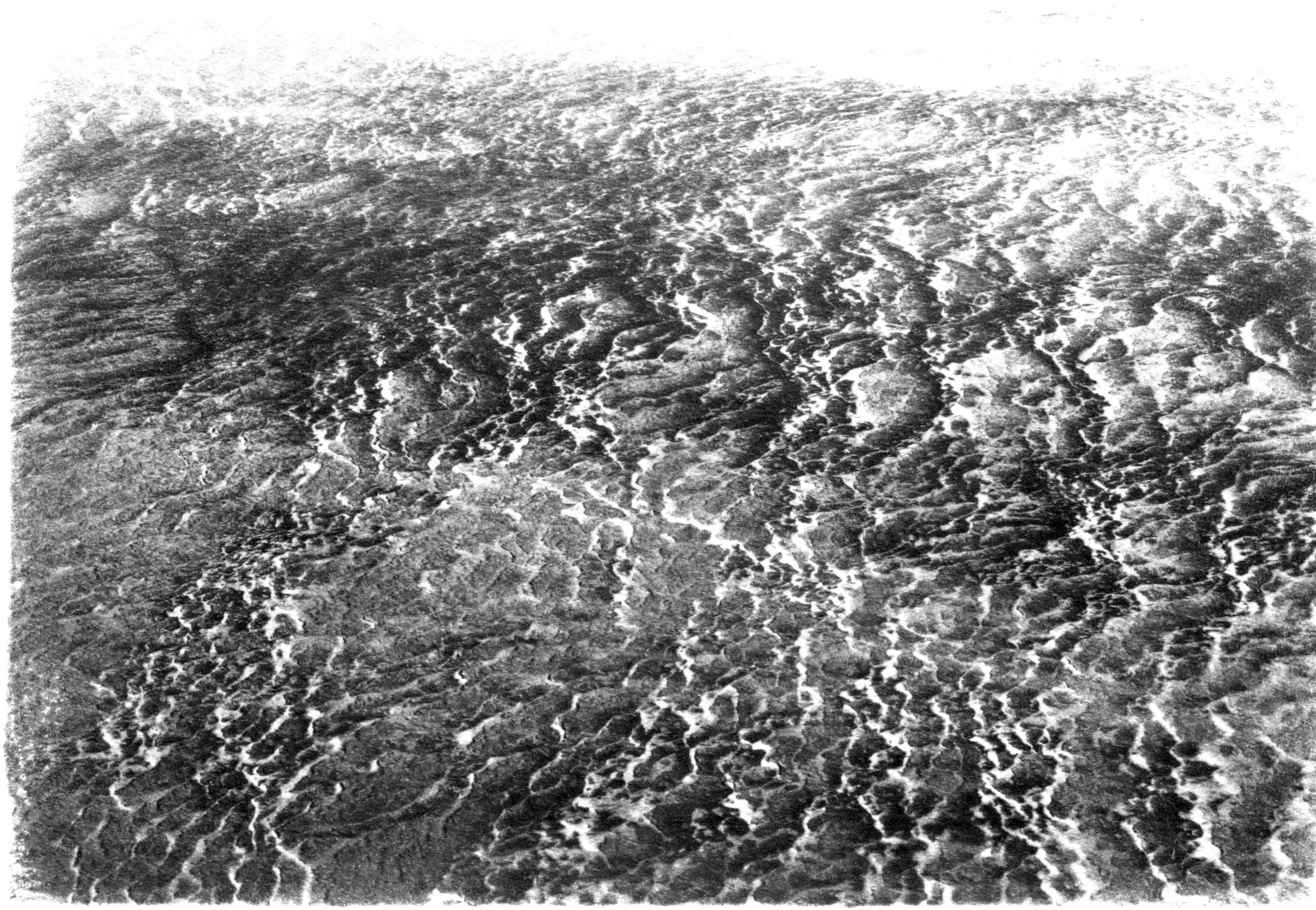

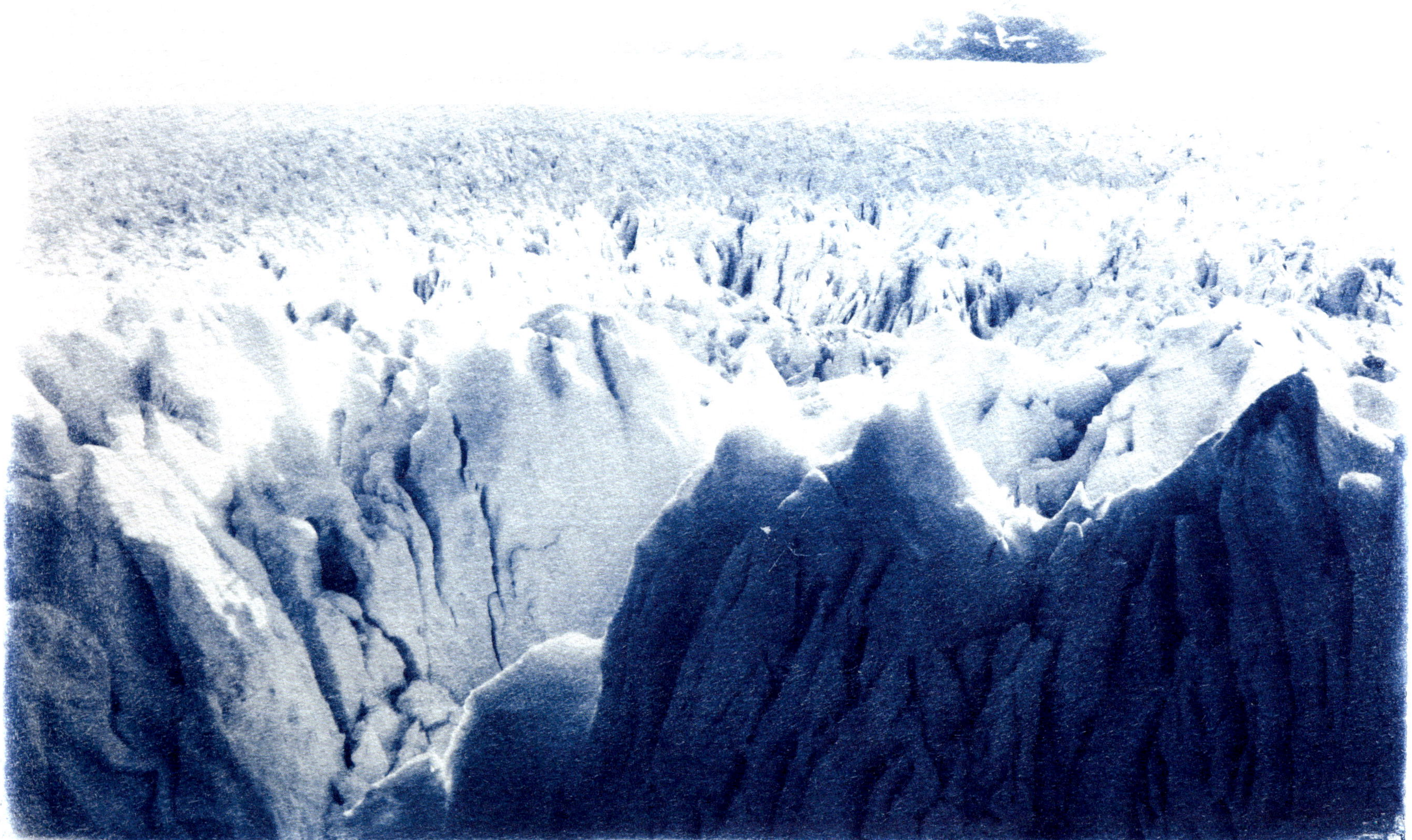

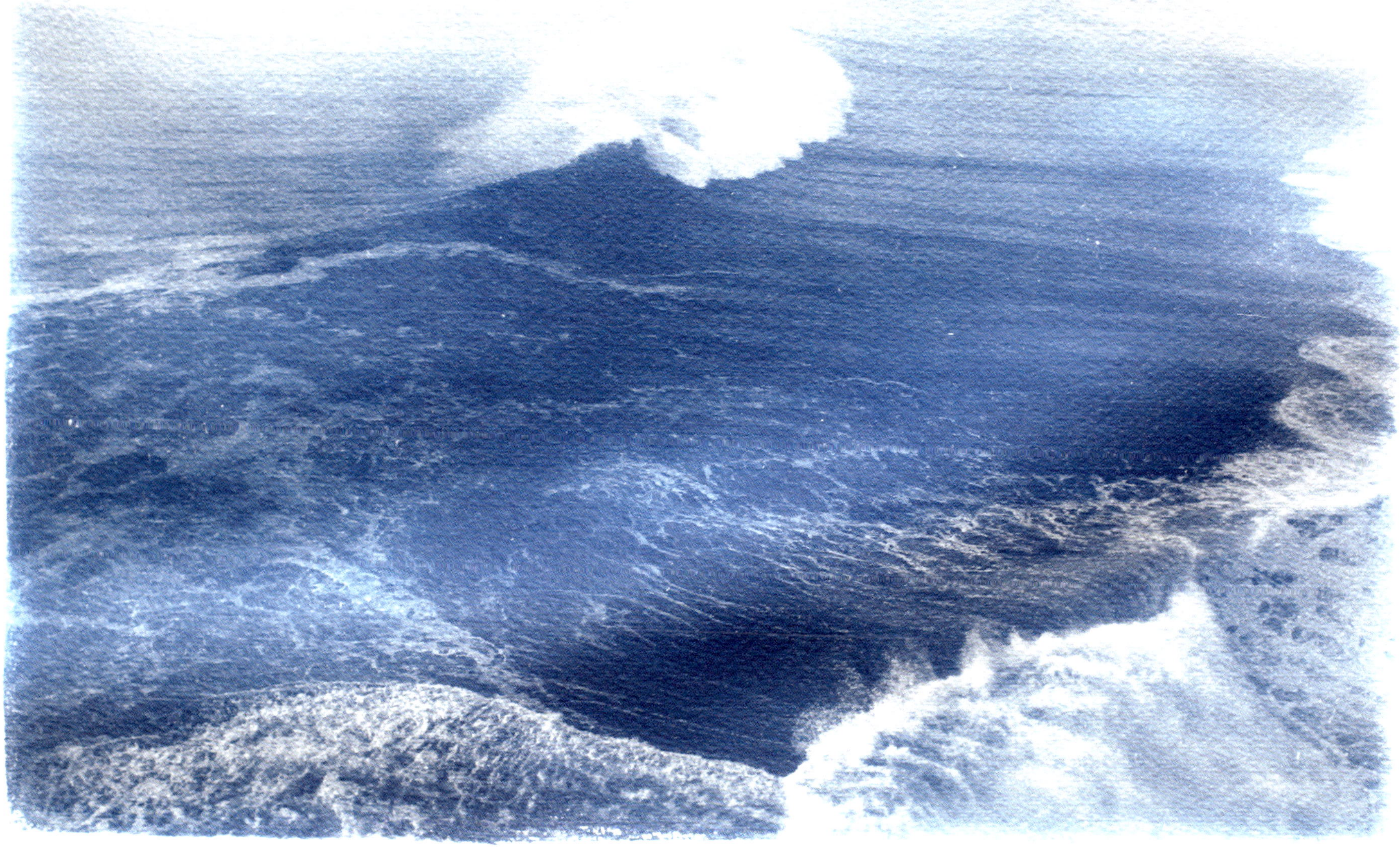

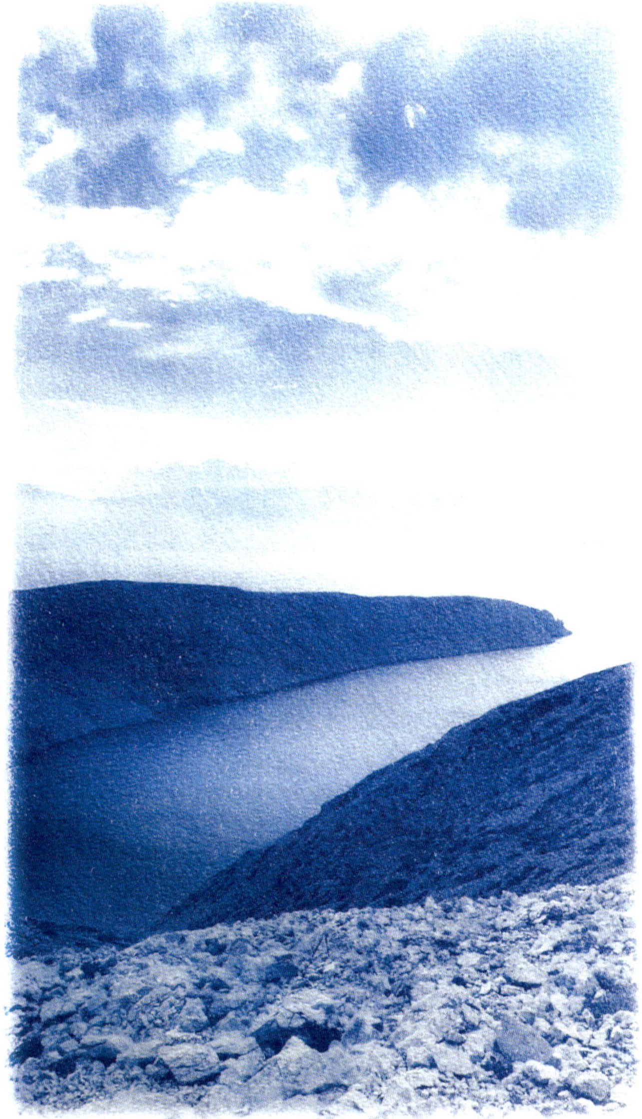

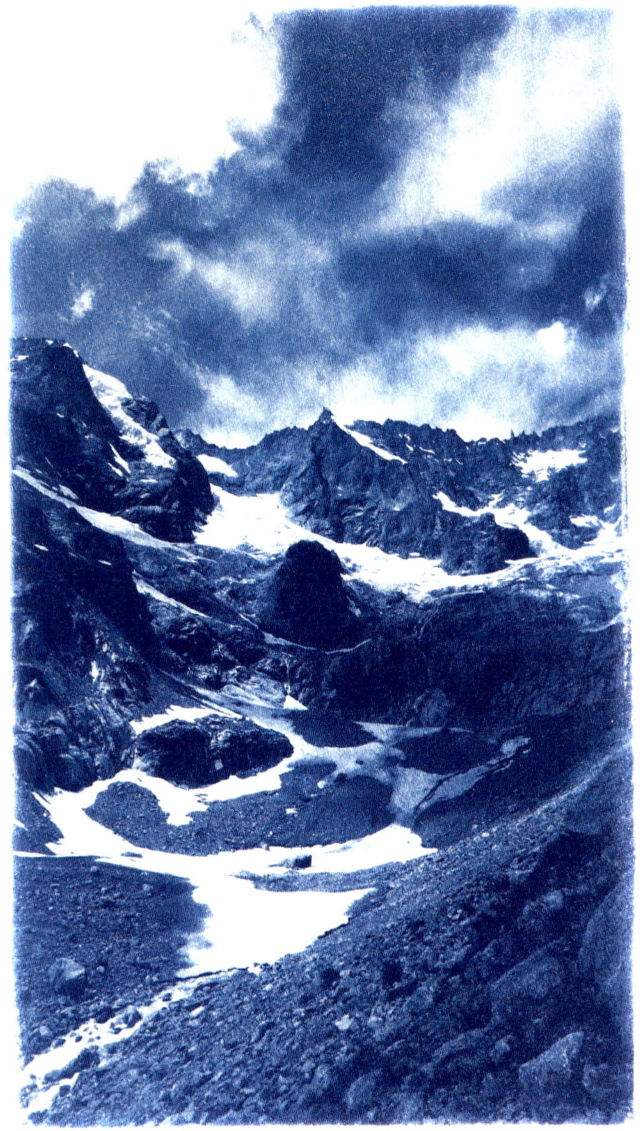

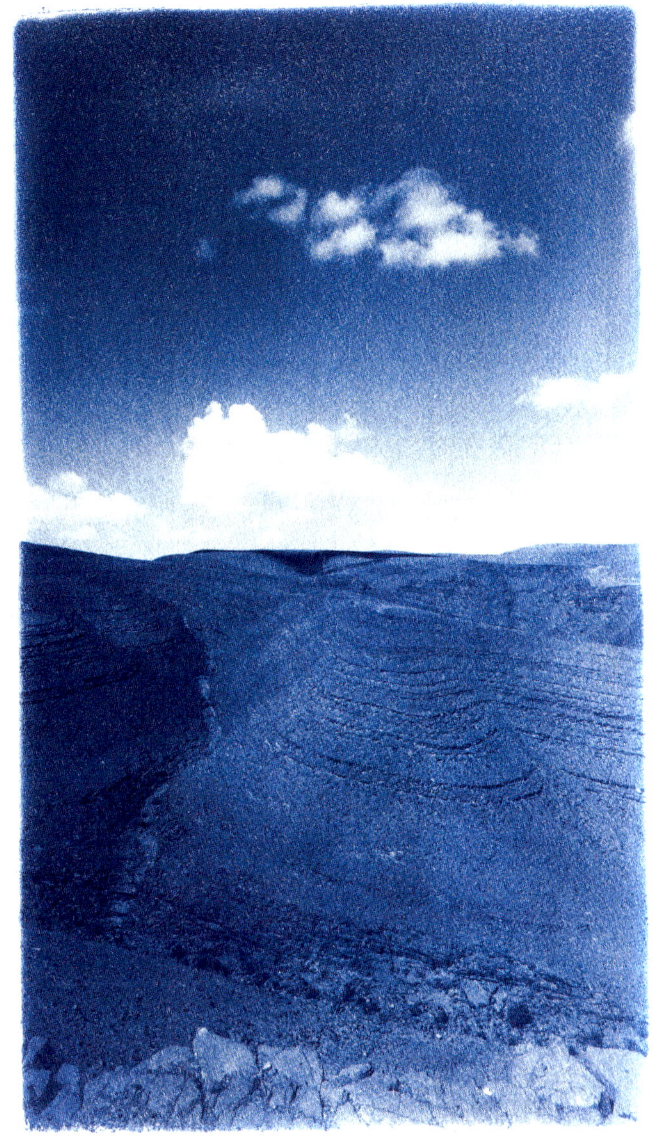

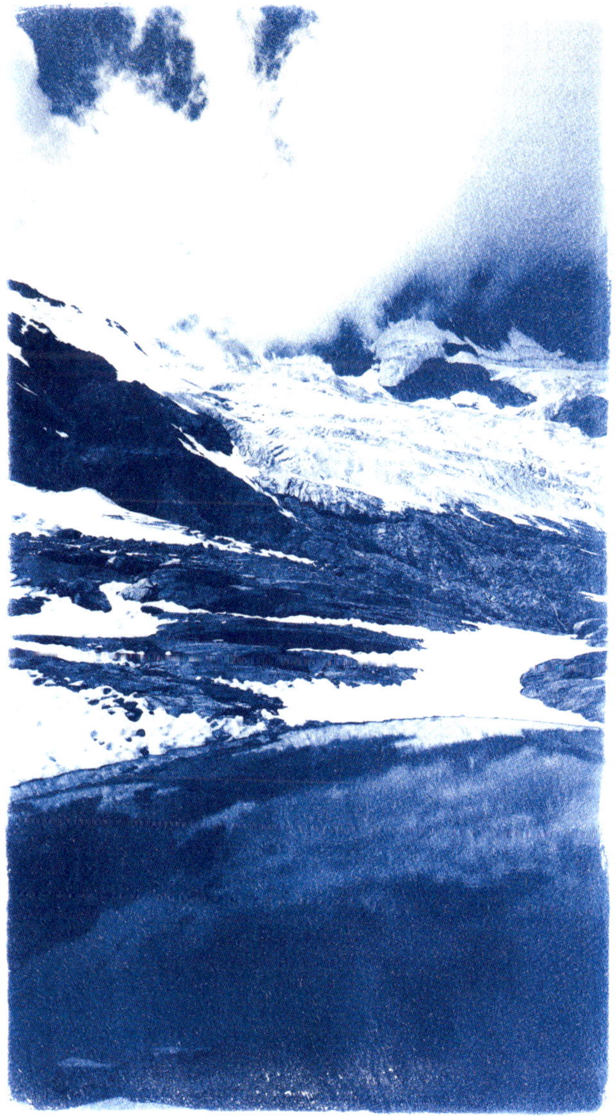
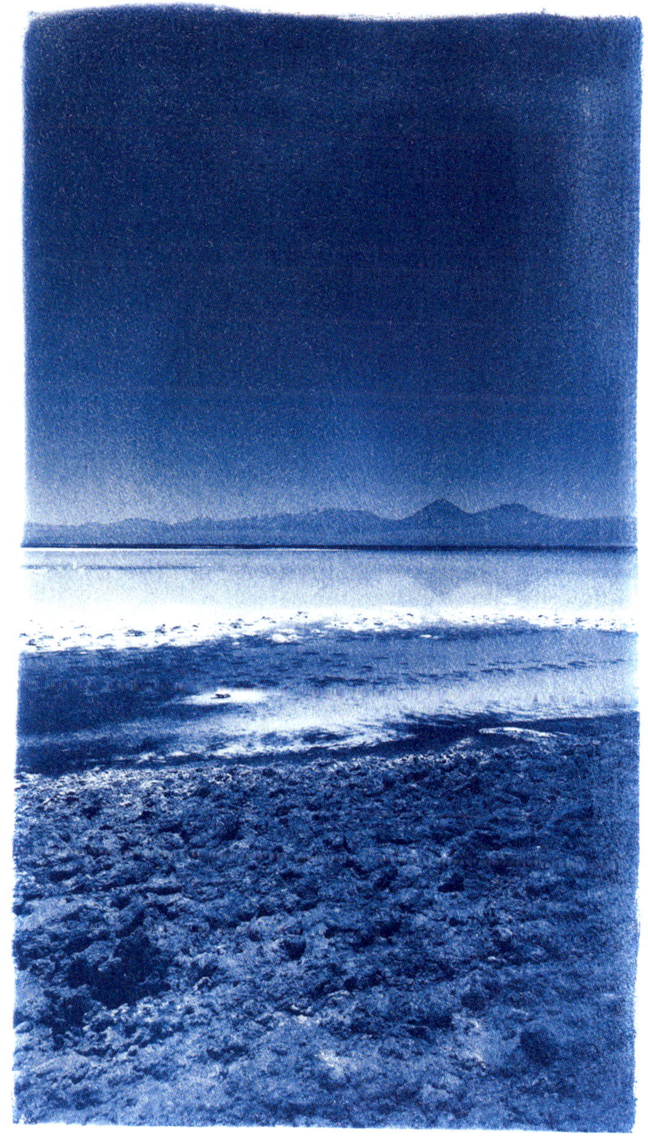

CRUX

Landschaft in Nahsicht mit der Konzentration auf das Wesentliche stand 2006 in der Ausstellung lauterland im Museum Pfalzgalerie Kaiserslautern im Blickpunkt. Der Fokus lag auf der Abbildung von Strukturen, die von Mensch und Maschine geschaffen wurden. Der Mensch selbst blieb außen vor. Kultur, lat. cultura, Bearbeitung, Pflege, Ackerbau von Nutzflächen, kreiert, wie Jörg Heieck, der kunstschaffende Fotograf in seinen Arbeiten beweist, hinreißende ästhetische Gebilde. Lineare und serielle Texturen wie Saatreihen und Ackerfurchen regen zum Nachdenken über die Schnittstellen und die gegenseitige Abhängigkeit von Mensch und Natur an.
Hier und heute in 2019 setzt der Fotograf, Physiker und Mensch Jörg Heieck in CRUX, lat. Kreuz, ungebändigten urbanen Kulturlandschaften, das heißt von Menschenhand gestalteten Straßenkreuzungen, Wüsten entgegen. Das sind unberührte vegetations- und menschenlose Trocken- oder Eisöden. Prototypen des Urzustands, die Lebenspotentiale für Pflanzen, Tiere und Menschen in sich bergen. Am Anfang war die Erde wüst und leer. Ihre Zukunft endet nach der creatio ex nihilo, wenn wir so weitermachen, für den Künstler Jörg Heieck nicht in blühenden oder gelobten Landschaften, sondern wieder in Ödnissen. Für Heieck ist die Wüste eine Metapher eines Raumes der Wachstumspotential für die Evolution birgt. Auf Grund des globalen ökologischen Raubbaus kann es nüchtern betrachtet mit der Bewahrung des Status quo oder einem Komme-was-wolle nicht weitergehen. Damit will er sich nicht zufriedengeben. Sein Anliegen ist, Augen zu öffnen und sichtbar zu machen: Was unsere Zukunft als auch die unseres Planeten angeht, stehen wir am Scheideweg.
Der vielreisende Fotograf durchstreift seit geraumer Zeit Großstädte der Welt. Unterwegs mit der Panoramakamera zielt er darauf ab, Schlüsselstellen des Lebens ausfindig zu machen und einzufangen. Das ist Fotografie, die ohne Inszenierung auskommt. Von besonderem Reiz sind für ihn die aus den vielfältigen Stadtlandschaften erwachsenen Bauformen und Lebensstile, also die besonderen Charakteristiken und Ausprägungen an urbanen Straßenkreuzungen und nicht der generische Raum. Heieck hat dabei immer sowohl den Menschen im Blick als auch den Kontext. Darunter fallen Dinge wie landestypische Schriftsysteme, Werbebanner, Plakate und Beschriftungen, alles, was ortsbedingte Besonderheiten und interessante Konfrontationen bietet. Jede Kultur hat ihr charakteristisches Abbildungssystem, ihre eigenen visuellen Merkmale und Codes. Die Schriften, Texte und Banner sind Begleiter, die in den urbanen Raum eingreifen und Aufschluss über kulturelle, soziale, ökonomische und gesellschaftliche Entwicklung geben. Sie sind Ausdruck eines Kultur-, Zeit- und Raumgeistes. Sie erzählen vom Leben, vom Konsum, dem Genuss und sonstigen materiellen Freuden des Daseins. Man kann die Spuren, die der Mensch hier hinterlässt, sehr unterschiedlich bewerten. Man kann sie als aufdringliche Zeichen lesen, die in die Ordnung städtischer Kulturlandschaften eingreifen und Architektur, Ästhetik und Gestaltung beschädigen. Man kann sie ebenso als kulturelle Wertobjekte betrachten und unter dem Begriff bereichernde stilistische Vielfalt subsumieren.
Heieck geht es primär nicht um eine schnelle, dynamische Reaktion auf aktuelle Ereignisse, sondern um das Aufspüren von epischen Perspektiven und Atmosphären. Intuitiv, so sagt er, erspürt er den geeigneten Standort, die Konstellationen der Dinge und Geschehnisse und ordnet, was er sieht. Auch der Künstler ist nicht durch und durch rational. Sein Auge wird dabei immer auch von innen geführt, einem Rückgriff auf sein geistiges Bildarchiv und dem individuellen Wechselspiel von rationalen Abwägungen, irrationalen Gegebenheiten und Emotionen.

Heieck richtet in seinen Panoramen den Fokus weniger in die Tiefe, denn in die Breite, nämlich auf die Vielfalt der Kontinente und Kulturen. Seine Fotografien sind primär keine Abbilder von eindeutig wiedererkennbaren Orten. Lebhaftes Treiben, geschäftiges Gedränge stehen für ihn nicht obenan, gleichwohl der Mensch hier die Feder führt. Der Künstler Jörg Heieck erhebt eher das Zufällige zum Exemplarischen und versucht dabei die jeweiligen kulturellen Eigenheiten einzufangen. Er kommt ohne jedwede Hinzufügung aus und zeigt in seinen ruhigen Bildern, dass in urbanen Räumen das Spezifische der Kulturen und die Bedingtheiten menschlichen Lebens sichtbar und manifest werden. Wir erfahren viel über ökonomische und interkulturelle Beeinflussungen und Überschneidungen als auch über das Ineinandergreifen von Fremdem und Eigenem.

Im Kontrast dazu stehen die faszinierenden anmutigen großformatigen Cyanotypien von öden Naturräumen. Das ist kreative Transformation von etwas, was für den Künstler Rohmaterial für die Evolution ist, aus anderer Perspektive wie Katastrophe aussieht. Sie macht uns bewusst, auf welch schmalen Grat wir wandeln. Von den überaus ästhetischen Trugbildern von mystischer Schönheit gehen Suggestivkräfte aus. Diese berühren die Frage: Welche menschlichen Lebensräume wollen wir. Daneben bieten sie Raum für Visionen und Dystopien.

Dass Bildende Kunst nicht nur mit den Augen und dem Verstand, sondern auch emotional wahrgenommen wird, das weiß der Physiker, gleichwohl er in seinem Fach wahrscheinlich der Ratio, will heißen Fakten, das letzte Wort zugestehen würde. Hier geht es ihm weder um das letzte Wort noch um die Machtfrage Verstand oder Gefühl, sondern darum, uns, den Betrachter, zum Innehalten, zur Achtsamkeit und zum Nachdenken zu bewegen.

In CRUX konfrontiert er uns mit seinem Entwurf von Zukunft aus der Vergangenheit, der auf der Idee beruht, dass der unheilvolle Kreis sich schließt. Wüste wird wieder zu Wüste. Welt hat einen Anfang und ein ebensolches Ende. Das lässt an Nietzsches ewige Wiederkehr der Dinge denken. In seinen Cyanotypien transformiert Heieck präzise Schwarz-Weiß-Aufnahmen von verödeten, vegetationslosen Gebieten. Mittels der Cyanotypie, einem alten fotografischen Druckverfahren, transportiert er Farbe und Unschärfe ins Papier und schafft so irritierend poetische Bilder. Was sich hier im Bild als ästhetische, kosmogenische Schöpfung darstellt, kann man als ein raffiniertes Spiel sehen, das uns zum Innehalten anhält und den Blick hinter die Kulissen fordert und uns die Möglichkeit bietet, sie für die Gegenwart zu befragen.

Wüsten werden hier nicht mehr nur dokumentiert, sondern inszeniert und neu geschaffen. Wüsten erscheinen vor unseren Augen als stille Oasen in Eisenblau. Räume der Imagination, die eisklare Botschaften von Schönheit und Erschrecken zugleich aussenden. Kultivierte Ästhetik holt uns auf den Boden der Tatsachen zurück und verweist auf die nüchtern und rational betrachtet existierende Bedrohung. Ins Blaue hinein weitermachen, das hieße unser aller Zukunft aufs Spiel zu setzen, das weiß er, das wissen wir. Hubert Portz

CRUX

The exhibition lauterland, shown at the museum Pfalzgalerie in Kaiserslautern, in 2006, focused on landscape in close up by concentrating on the fundamental. The center of attention was the depiction of patterns, which were created by humans and machines. Nevertheless, humans themselves remained absent here. Culture, in Latin cultura, process, treatment, and cultivation of farmland create as Jörg Heieck, the photographer, depicts in his work fascinating aesthetic formations. Linear and serial textures such as seeding rows and furrows encourage one to contemplate the interfaces of human and nature.

In 2019, Heieck, the photographer, physicist, and human being, contrasts untamed urbanscapes; man-made, designed intersections, against desertscapes. These are untouched, barren and uninhabited dry or frozen wastelands; prototypes of the original state, containing the potential for vegetation, animals, and humans.

In the beginning, the earth was desolate and empty. In Heieck's opinion, the future of the planet ends, in accordance with the creatio ex nihilo, not in flourishing and thriving landscapes, but in wastelands, should we continue our way of life. In Heieck's eyes, the desert is a metaphor for locality, with the potential for growth of the evolution. With global ecological exploitation in mind, the perspective of the preservation of the status quo or the "no-matter-what" cannot continue. The artist will not be satisfied with this. His concern is to open one's eyes and reveal that we are at a crossroads, for our future and the future of our planet.

The peripatetic photographer has been wandering through cities of this world for some time. On the go with his panorama camera, he searches for vantages to capture life. This is photography which manages without staging. Of particular interest to him are the diverse city landscapes created by architecture and lifestyle; thus, the individual qualities and manifestations of urban intersections, and not generic spaces.

Heieck always focuses on the human as well as the contextual. These include elements such as vernacular writing, advertising banners, posters, and labels, everything that offers local characteristics and exciting confrontations. Every culture has its unique imaging system, its own visual features, and codes. Script, texts, and banners are companions that intervene in the urban space and provide insight into cultural, social, ecological, and societal development. They are an expression of the cultural, temporal, and spatial spirit of their age. They tell stories of life, consumption, pleasures, and other material joys of existence. One can evaluate the traces, which humans leave behind, very differently. One can read them as intrusive signs, that interfere with the order of the urbanscape, damaging architecture, aesthetics, and design. One can similarly regard these traces as valuable cultural objects, subsumed in the concept of enriched stylistic diversity.

Heieck does not primarily pursue a fast, dynamic reaction to current events, but rather a tracing of narrative perspectives and atmospheres. He intuitively, as he remarks, senses the suitable location, the constellation of things and events and arranges what he sees. Moreover, the artist is not entirely rational. His eye is always lead from within, relying on a recourse to his mental image archive as well as the personal interaction of rational thoughts and irrational circumstances and emotions.

Heieck focuses on width rather than depth in his panoramic views, namely, the abundance of continents and cultures. His photographs primarily do not depict specific and recognizable places. Human liveliness is not the prime focus in his work, even though the human being is ultimately responsible. The artist Heieck instead elevates the coincidental as the exemplary and tries to capture particular cultural peculiarities. He works minimally and demonstrates in his urbanscapes the uniqueness of cultures and the evanescence of human life. We encounter plenty of economic and intercultural influences and overlappings, as well as the meshing of the strange and familiar, in his urbanscapes.

The fascinating and large format cyanotypes of dreary natural environments mark a contrast to these. From the artist's perspective, this creative transformation of the barren is raw material for evolution, while on the other hand, it evokes catastrophe. We are made aware of the tightrope we are walking on. Ideas of the sublime originate from the mirage of mystical beauty. These touch upon the question: What human habitats do we seek? At the same time, they make room for visions and dystopias.

Art is not only perceived through the eye and mind but also through emotions, as is apparent to the physicist, although he would grant the last words to physics´ deductive logic, namely, the facts. Here he does not concentrate on the last words nor the question of the power of reason or emotion but rather seeks to move us, the observer, to pause, to be mindful and contemplate.

In CRUX, he confronts us with his design of a future derived from the past, where this sinister cycle ends. Desert again becomes desert. The world has a beginning and also an end. This reminds us of Nietzsche's idea of eternal return. In his cyanotypes, Heieck transforms the precise black and white photos of desolate and barren areas. With the help of cyanotype, an old photographic printing technique, he introduces color and intentional lack of focus to paper and creates provocative, poetic photos. What we see here is a beautiful cosmogenic creation, a refined performance, which asks for us to look behind the scenes, giving us the possibility to question the present. Deserts are no longer documented but staged and newly created.

Deserts appear as calm oases in Prussian blue to our eye - spaces for imagination that emit crystal-clear messages of beauty and horror. When regarded rationally and soberly, Heieck's cultivated aesthetic brings us back down to earth to realize the overwhelming, existing threat. To continue into the blue would mean to jeopardize all of our future; he is aware of this as well are we. Hubert Portz

Jörg Heieck

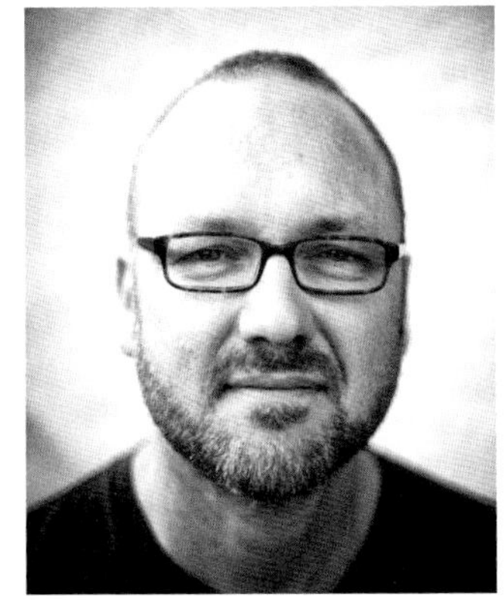

geboren in Münster 1964, aufgewachsen in Otterbach, ist Künstler und promovierter Physiker. Er studierte Physik, Mathematik und Philosophie in Frankfurt (bei F. Granzer) und Edinburgh (P. Higgs), finanziert mit Jazz und Bierzeltmusik.
Als Wissenschaftler war er mehrere Jahre für Agfa, Kodak und das ITER Kernfusionsprojekt der Europäischen Kommission in Italien tätig, 1995 wurde er mit dem ITEK Award der amerikanischen Gesellschaft für Imaging Science ausgezeichnet.
Heieck ist Vater zweier erwachsener Kinder und lebt in Kaiserslautern. Dort lehrt er Physik und Photographie. Seine Arbeiten werden im In- und Ausland ausgestellt und befinden sich in öffentlichen und privaten Sammlungen. Er kuratiert und betreibt den Brownian Motion Art Space und engagiert sich in regionalen Kulturprojekten (Pfaffwerk Kaiserslautern, Pixxelcult Saarbrücken). Heieck ist Autor vieler Bildbände und berufenes Mitglied der Deutschen Gesellschaft für Photographie (DGPh).

was born in Münster (1964) and grew up in Otterbach. The artist holds a Ph.D. in physics and studied in Frankfurt under F. Granzer and in Edinburgh under P. Higgs. In order to pay for his studies of physics, mathematics and philosophy, Heieck performed Jazz and "Bierzeltmusik" (German folk music).
For several years he worked as a scientist for Agfa, Kodak and the ITER nuclear fusion research project for the European Commission in Italy. In 1995, he received the ITEK award by the American Society for Imaging Sciences.
Heieck is a father of two adult children and lives in Kaiserslautern. There he teaches physics and photography. His works have been shown worldwide and are part of public and private collections. He curates and manages the Brownian Motion Art Space and is involved in regional, cultural projects such as Pfaffwerk Kaiserslautern, Pixxelcult Saarbrücken. Heieck is the author of many photo publications and an appointed member of the German Society for Photography (DGPh).

Ausstellungsauswahl | Exhibitions

1996 Theodor-Zink-Museum Kaiserslautern
1998 Photokina Köln
1999 Goethe Institut Damaskus, Photo Festival Aleppo
2000 Goethe Institut Beirut, Villa Strecchius Landau
2001 Galerie Grauwert Hamburg
2002 Universidad Santiago de Chile, Volksbank Kaiserslautern
2003 DAAD Cairo
2004 Kunstverein Speyer, Walser Herbst Blons
2005 Landesvertretung Rheinland-Pfalz Berlin, Kunsthalle Mannheim
2006 Museum Pfalzgalerie Kaiserslautern, Museum im Westrich Ramstein
2007 Linhof München, Thermen am Viehmarkt Trier
2008 Cité de l'image Clervaux
2009 Wilhelm-Hack-Museum Ludwigshafen, Villa Ruh Zingst
2011 Architekturgalerie Kaiserslautern
2012 Casa Bertold Brecht Montevideo, Centro Cultural Porto Alegre, if art Gallery Columbia
2013 Art El Lewa Gallery Cairo
2014 Stadtmuseum Zweibrücken, Frank-Loebsches Haus Landau
2016 Museum Pfalzgalerie Kaiserslautern, Zehnthaus Jockgrim
2017 Museum Pachen Rockenhausen
2019 Galerie Decumanus Krk, Eisfabrik Offenbach

Technik

Die Cyanotypien im ersten Teil sind Kontaktabzüge von digitalen Grossnegativen auf Hahnemühle Aquarellpapier. Seit 2005 sind sie u. a. in der Sahara, Island, Spitzbergen, Arizona und den Anden entstanden. Die Hauptserie hat das Format 27x40cm (Papierbogen 50x65cm). Die Arbeiten im Seitenverhältnis 1:2 haben die Maße 42x90cm (65x100cm). Die hochformatigen Cyanotypien mit 40x22cm (65x50cm) wurden mit der ProCamera App erstellt.
Die Strassenkreuzungsbilder wurden seit dem Jahr 1998 mit einer analogen Linhof 617 Super Angulon 5,6/72mm Panoramakamera aufgenommen. In den letzten Jahren wurde zusätzlich mit einer digitalen Canon 5Ds Kamera und Irix 2,4/15mm Optik mit gleichem Bildwinkel photographiert. Die Standardgröße der Abzüge ist 15x42cm auf Barytpapier, einige Arbeiten wurden auf Aludibond bis 60x140cm vergrößert.

Technical notes

The cyanotypes in the first part of the book are contact prints of large-format negatives on Hahnemühle paper. Since 2005, they have been photographed in the Sahara Desert, Iceland, Spitzbergen, Arizona, and the Andes. The main series has a format of 27x40 cm (paper sheet 50x65cm). Other works have an aspect ratio 1:2 and the format of 42x90 cm (65x100cm). The vertically oriented cyanotypes with 40x22cm (65x50cm) were made with the ProCamera App.
Starting in 1998, the photographs of urbanscapes were taken with an analog Linhof 617 Super Angulon 5,6/72mm panoramic camera. In recent years, photographs were also taken with the digital Canon 5Ds camera with an Irix 2,4/15mm lens and the same viewing angle. The standard size for prints is 15x42cm on fiber-base paper; some works were enlarged on dibond panels up to 60x140cm.

Ausstellungen / Exhibitions	Kunsthaus Désirée Hochstadt	01.09. - 29.09.2019
	Kunstverein Neustadt/Weinstrasse	15.11. - 01.12.2019

Besonderer Dank an: Ray Albuquerque, Bernd Barde, Ina Bartenschlager, Nicolai Bönig, Jens Daemgen, Dr. Christoph Dammann, Dr. Ulrike Dittberner, Gordon Drummond, Katrin Fechner, Michael Fetzer, Andreas Fillibeck, Clovis Freire, Kai Gundacker, Werner Heckmann, Duncan Heieck, Elfi Heieck, Fiona Heieck, Richard Heieck, Lance Hewison, Katrin Hiestand, Dr. Heinz Höfchen, Markus Kaesler, Gabi Kaiser, Tinatin Kiguradze, Jochen Kitzbihler, Prof. Sebastian Kraus, Dr. Fabian Lovisa, Markus Lücke, Christian Müksch, Richard Müller, Werner Mummert, Prof. Dr. Helmut Neunzert, Susanne Ossendorf, Dr. Hubert Portz, Hamdy Reda, Miriam Roath, Norbert Roth, Victor Senkov, Patricia Weiss, Günther Wilhelm

Text: Hubert Portz
Übersetzung: Miriam Roath
Gestaltung: Jörg Heieck
Druck: Dr. Cantz´sche Druckerei Medien GmbH Esslingen
ISBN 978-3-947563-49-4

Hauptsponsor: Kunsthaus Désirée Hochstadt
Unterstützer: Kunstverein Neustadt/Weinstrasse, ProCamera Mannheim

heieck.net
kunsthaus-desiree.de
kunstverein-nw.de
procamera-app.com
edition-cantz.de

für Duncan und Fiona

edition cantz

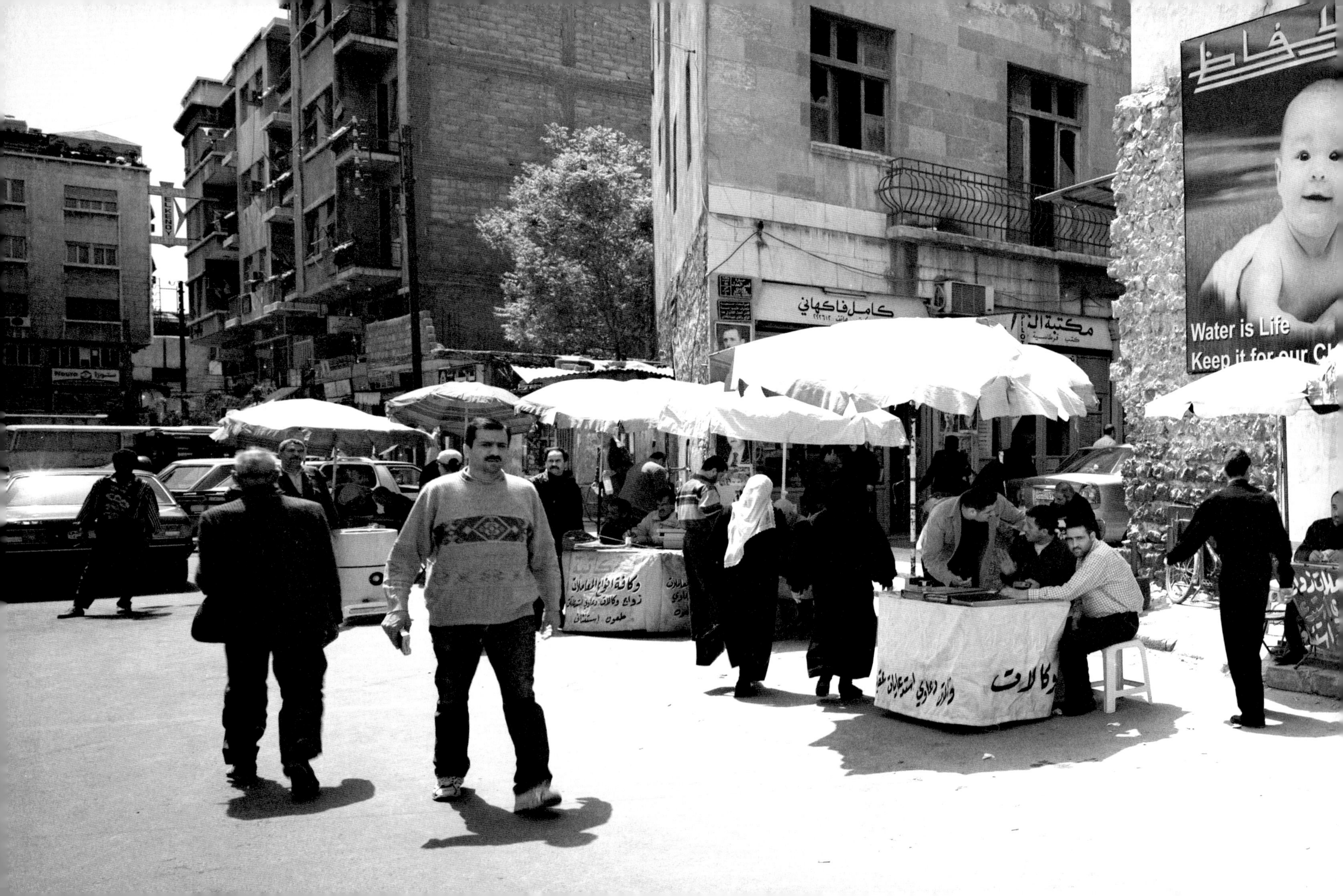
كامل فاكهاني
Water is Life
Keep it for our

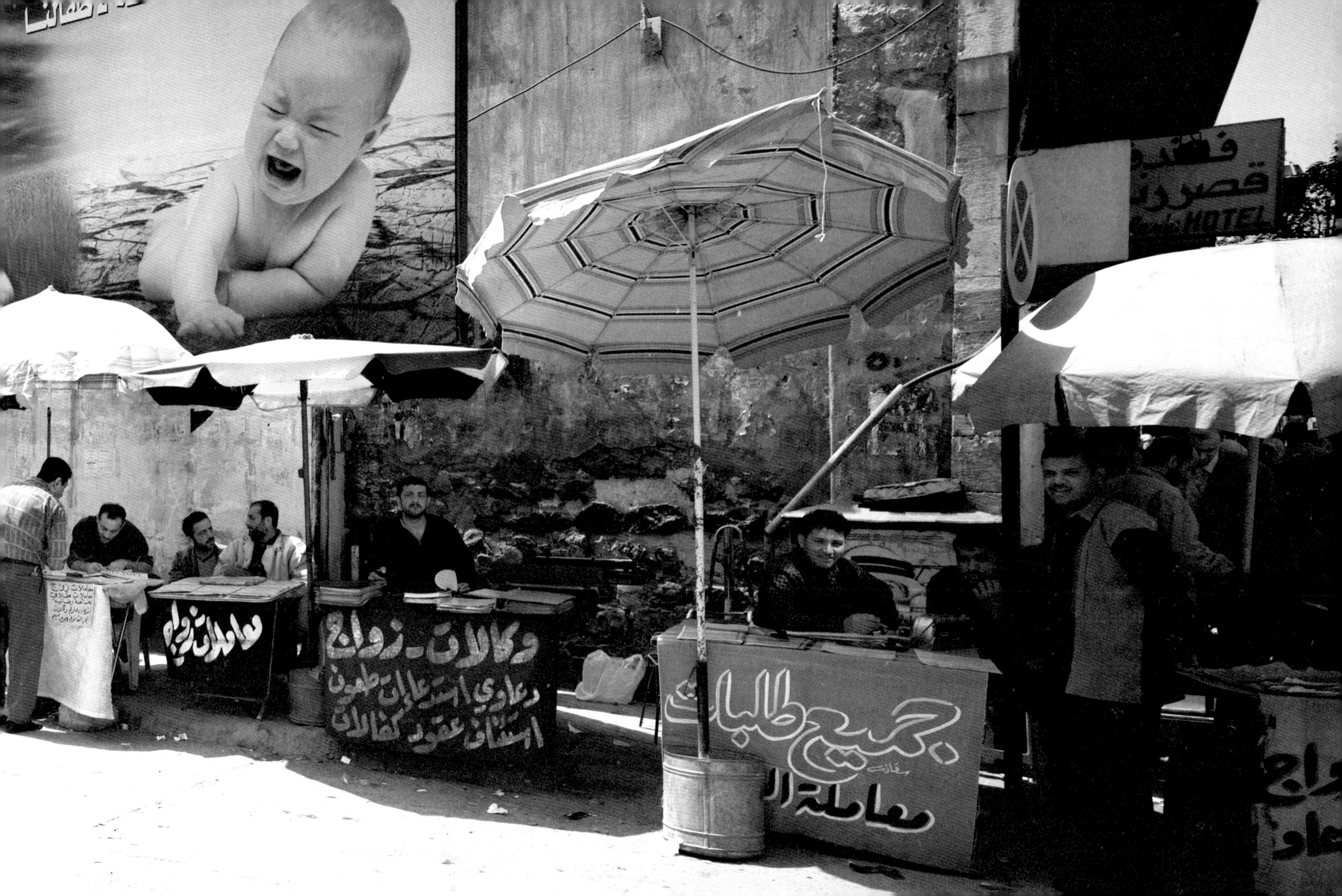
HOTEL
معاملات زواج
وكالات - زواج
جميع طلبات

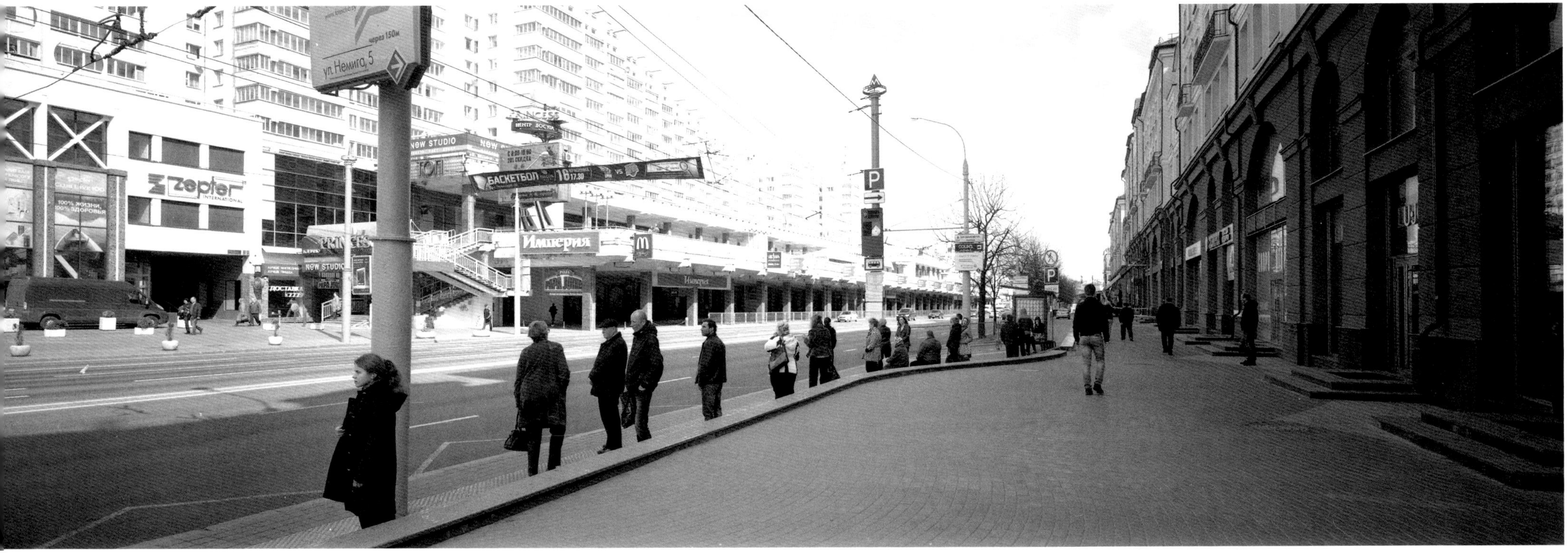

Minsk 2017

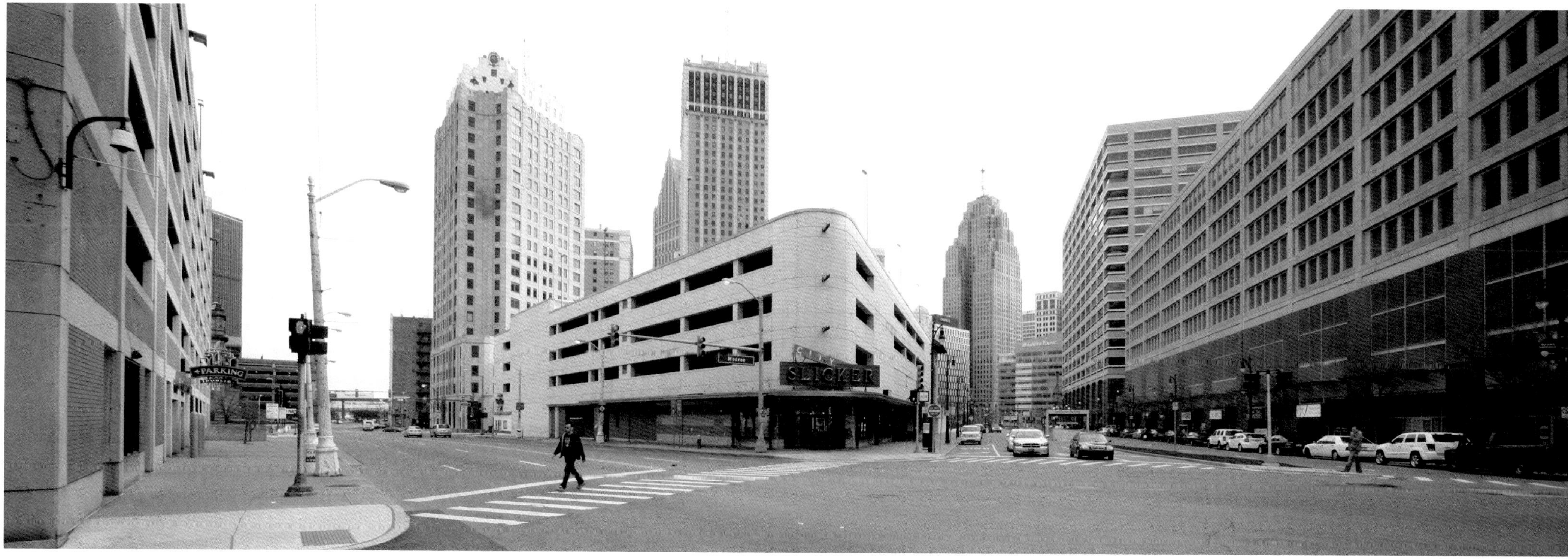

Detroit 2011

< Damascus 2001

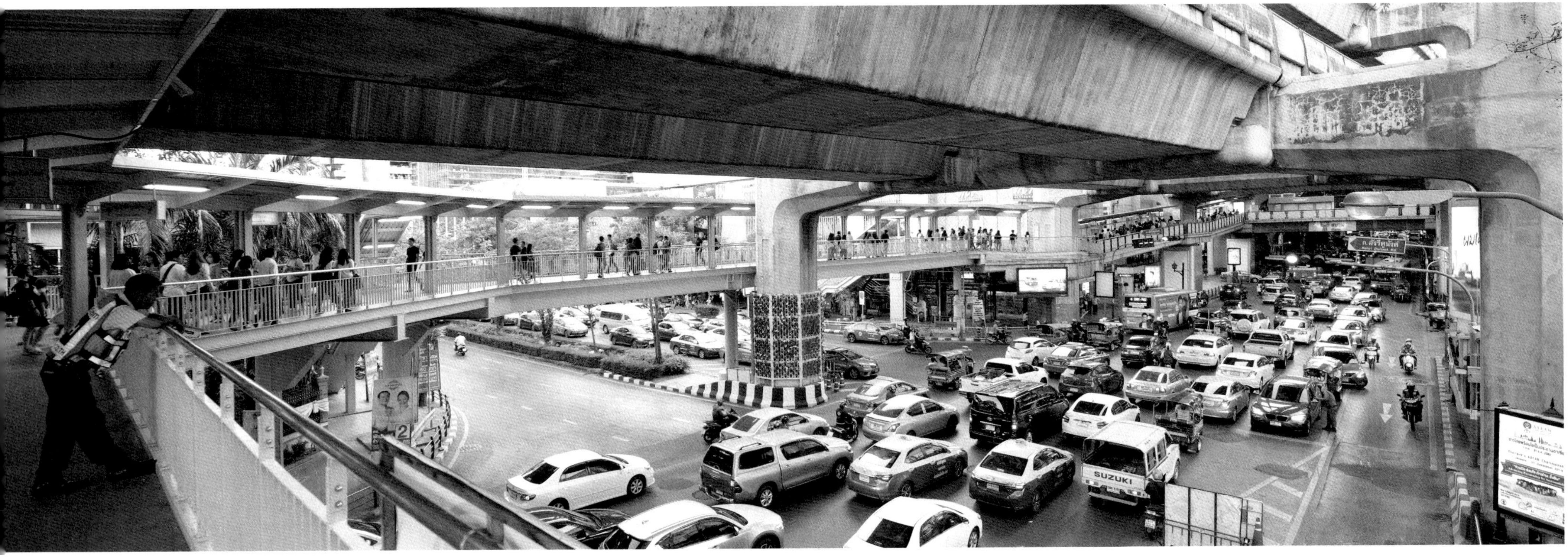

Bangkok 2019

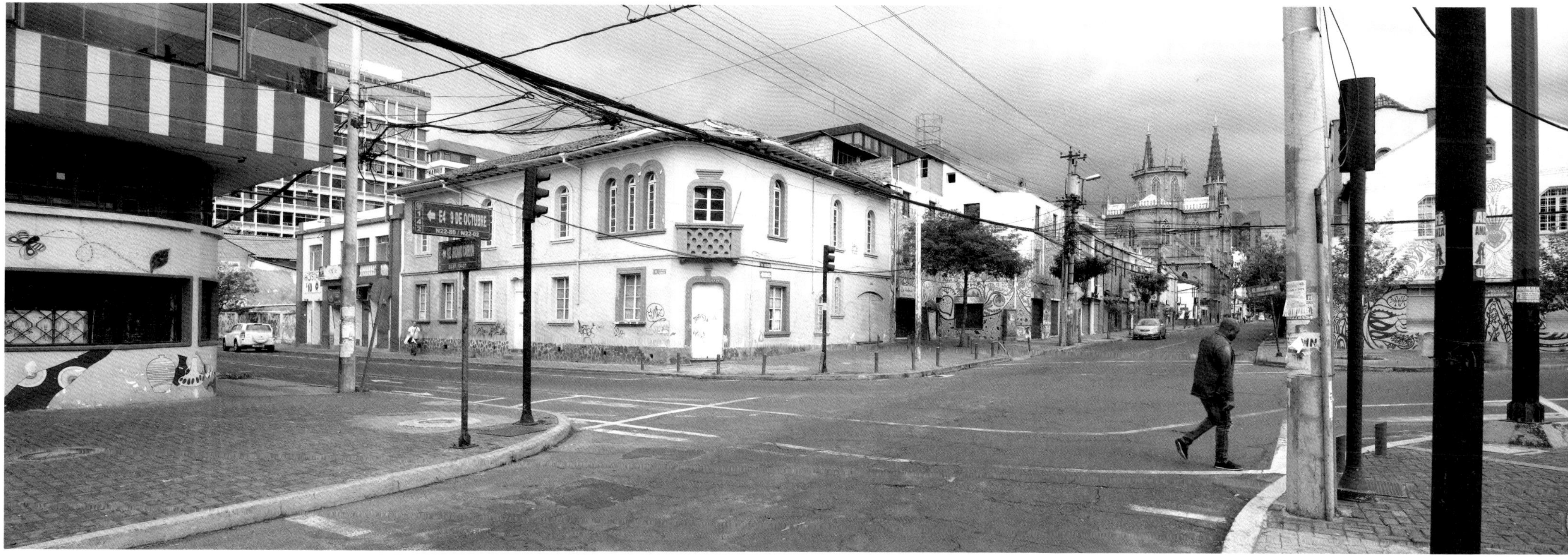

Quito 2018

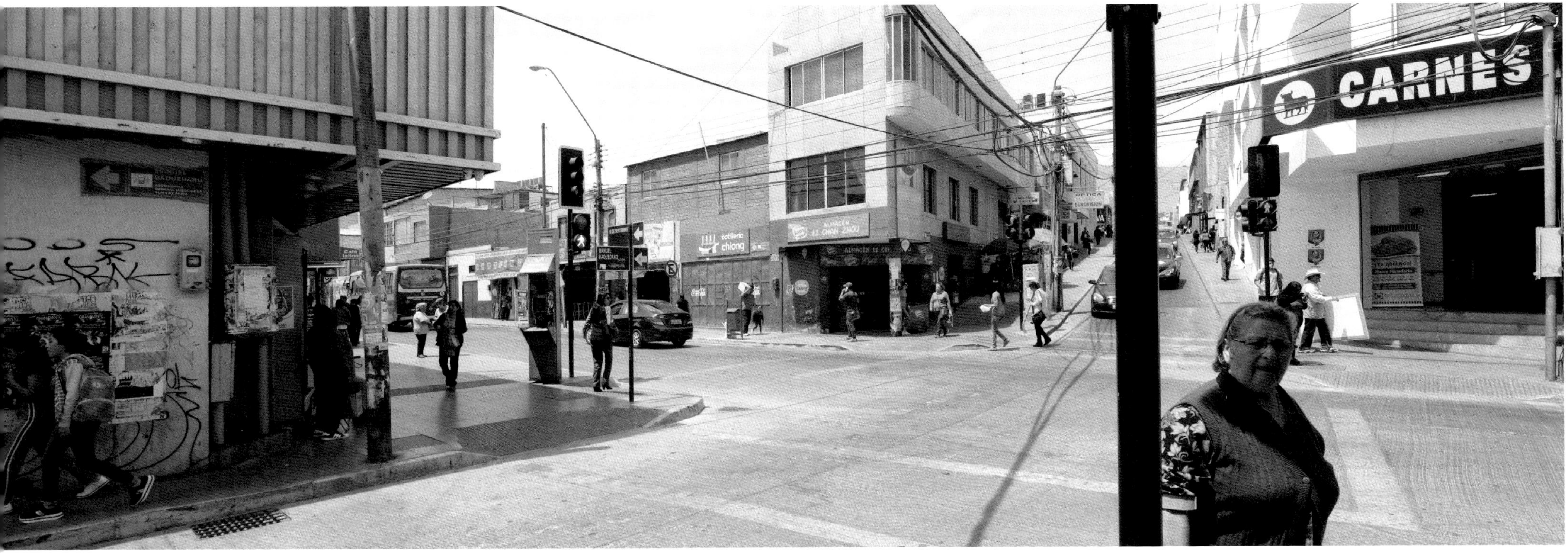

Arica 2018

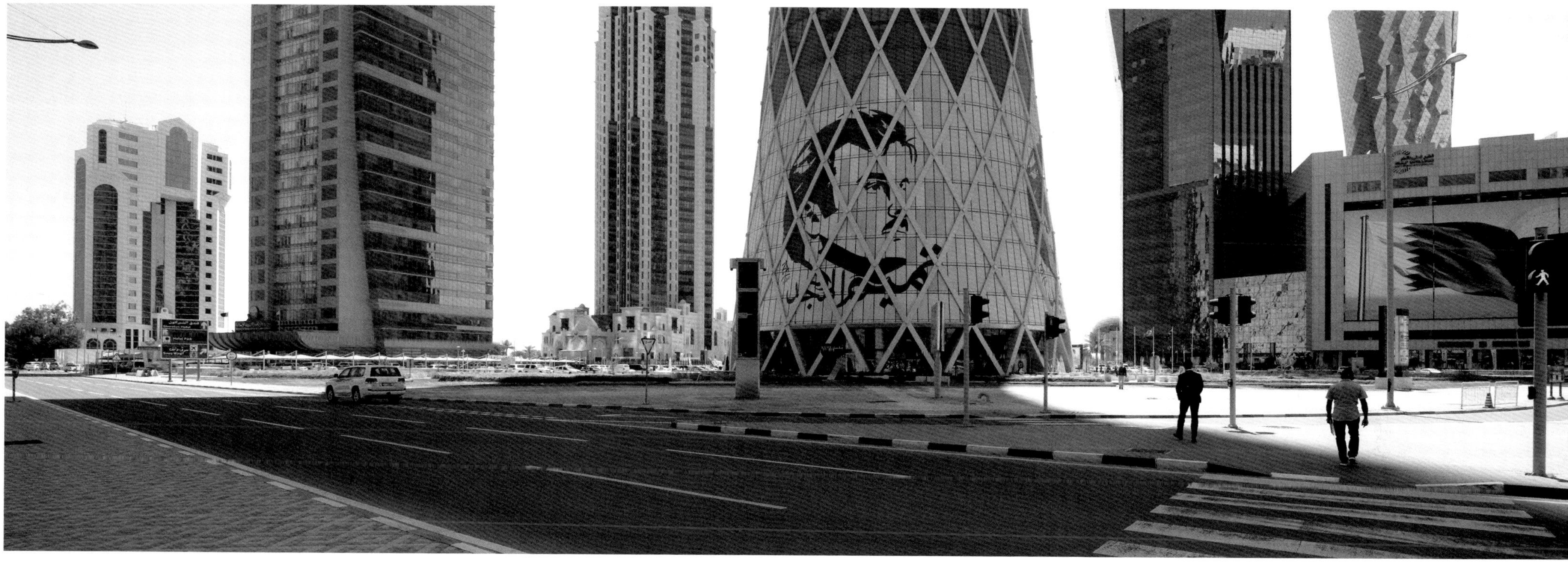

Doha 2019

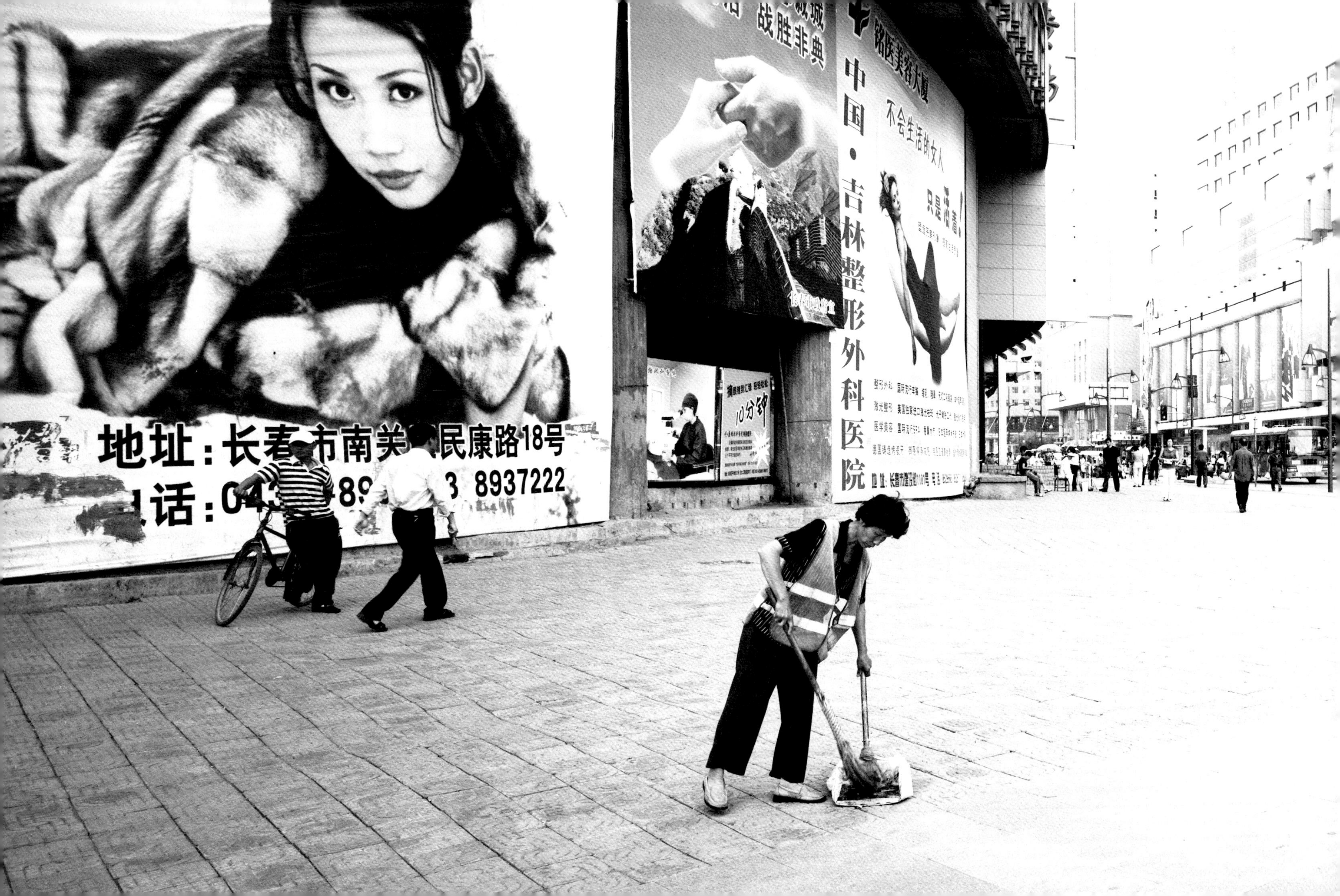
地址：长春 市南关 民康路18号
话：043 89 3 8937222
战胜非典
铭医美容大厦
中国·吉林整形外科医院
不会生活的女人

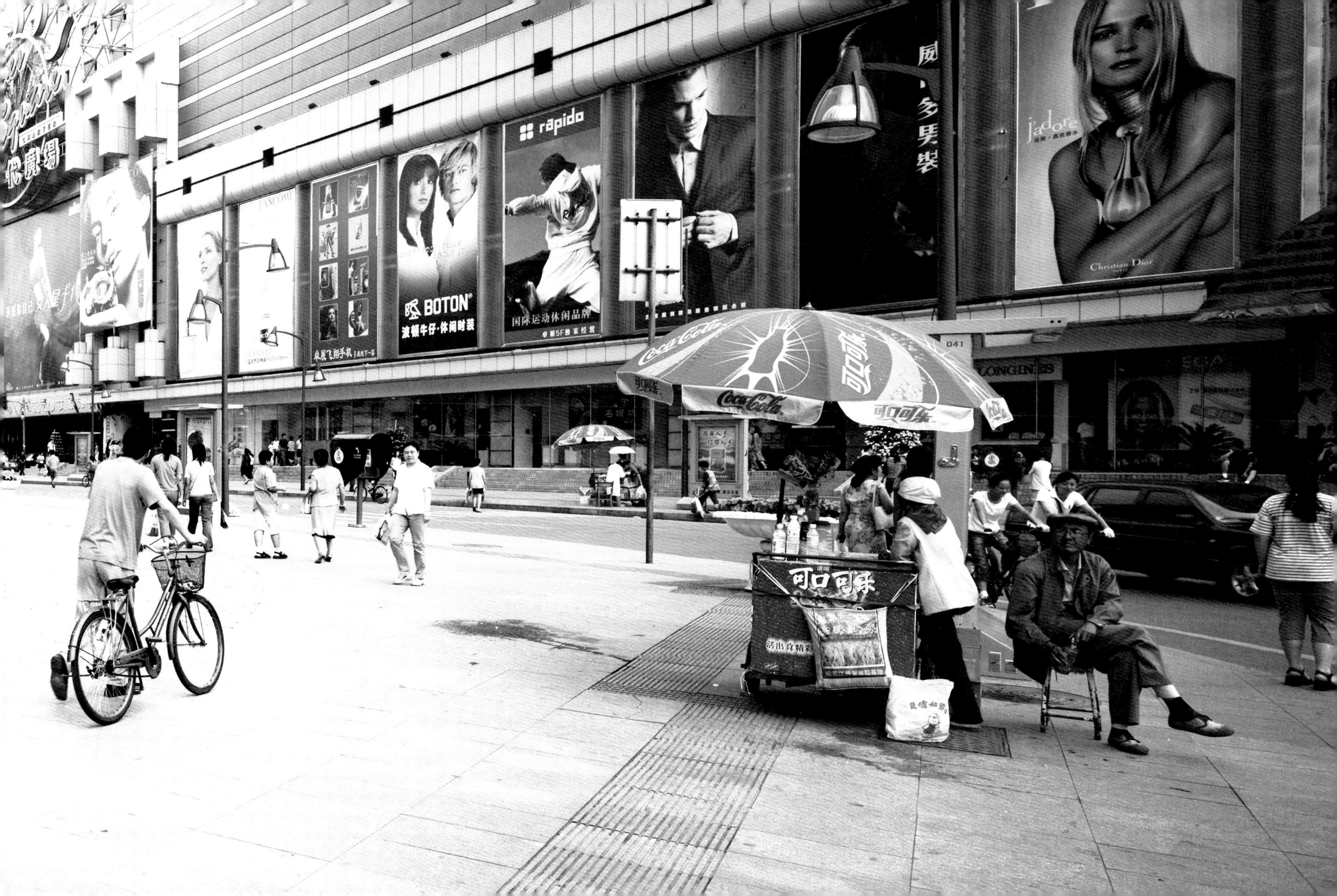
rapido
国际运动休闲品牌
BOTON®
波顿牛仔·休闲时装
卓展飞翔手机
LANCOME
j'adore
Christian Dior
LONGINES
Coca-Cola
可口可乐
可口可乐

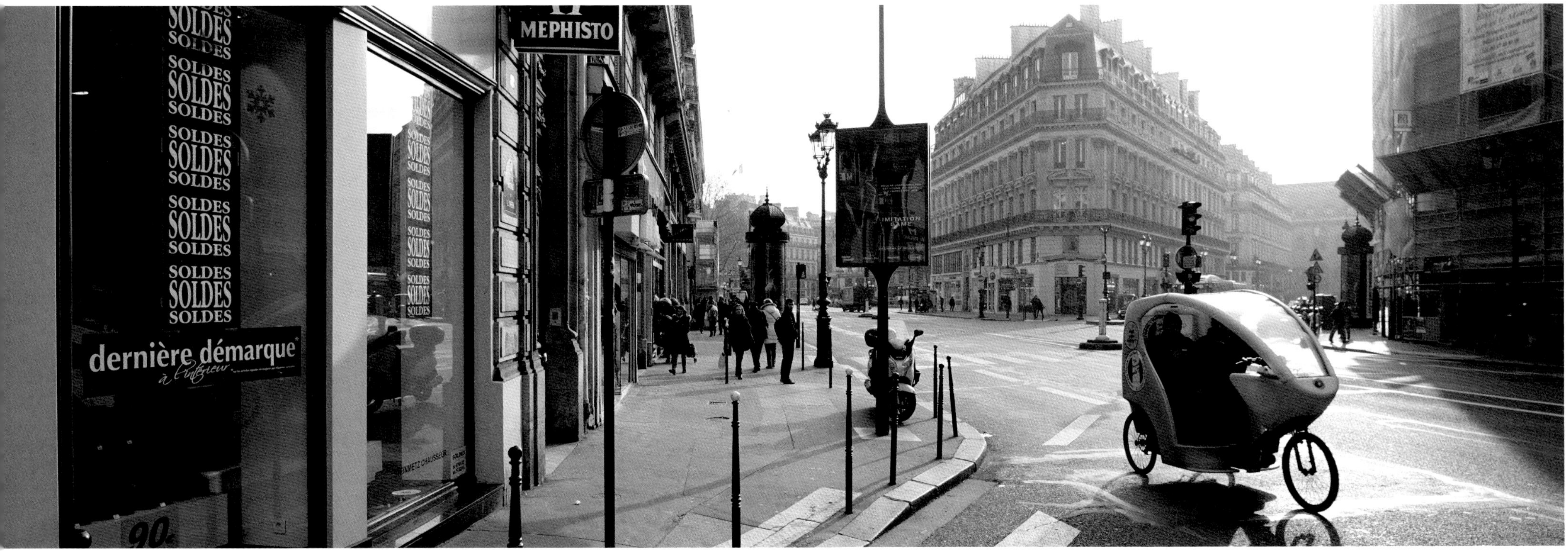
SOLDES
SOLDES
SOLDES
MEPHISTO
dernière démarque*
à l'intérieur
IMITATION GAME

Paris 2015

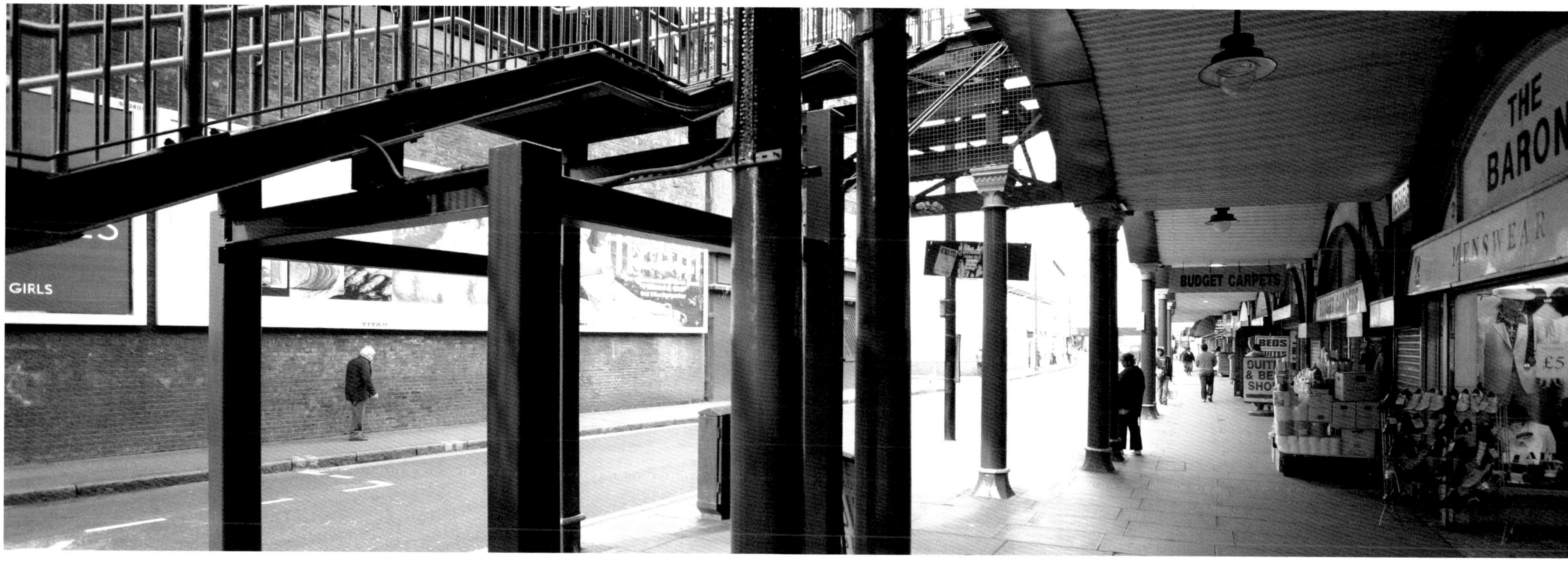

London 2008

< Changchun 2003

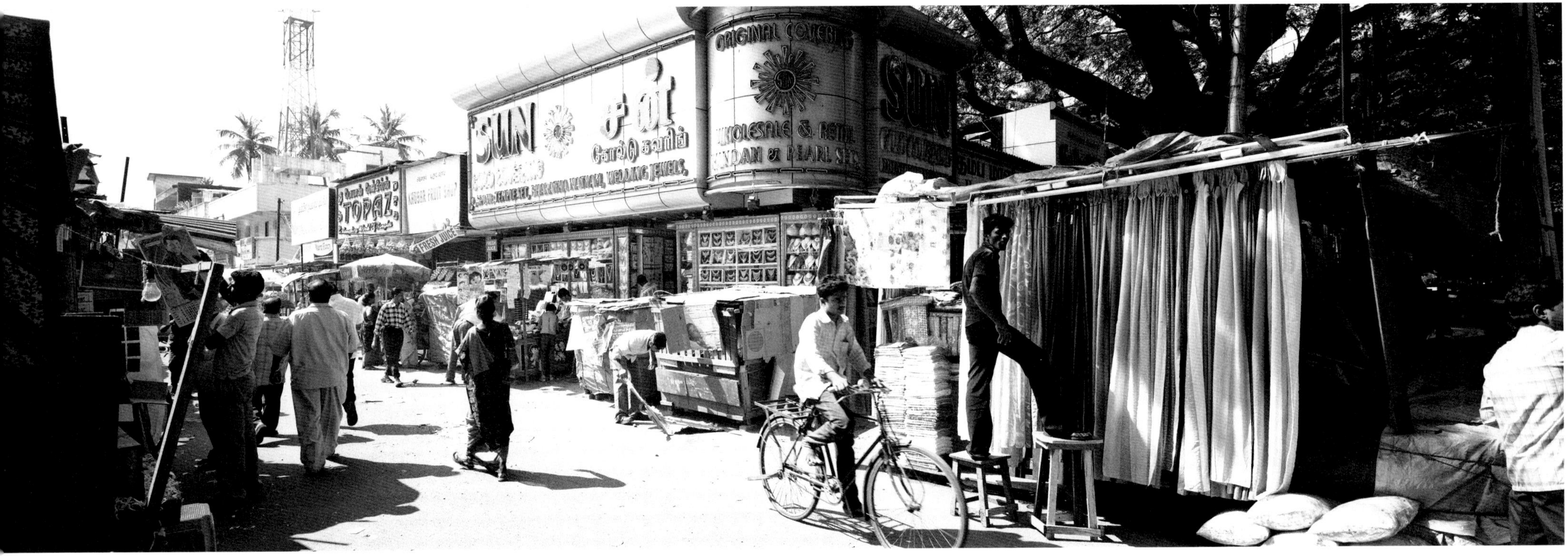

Chennai 2008

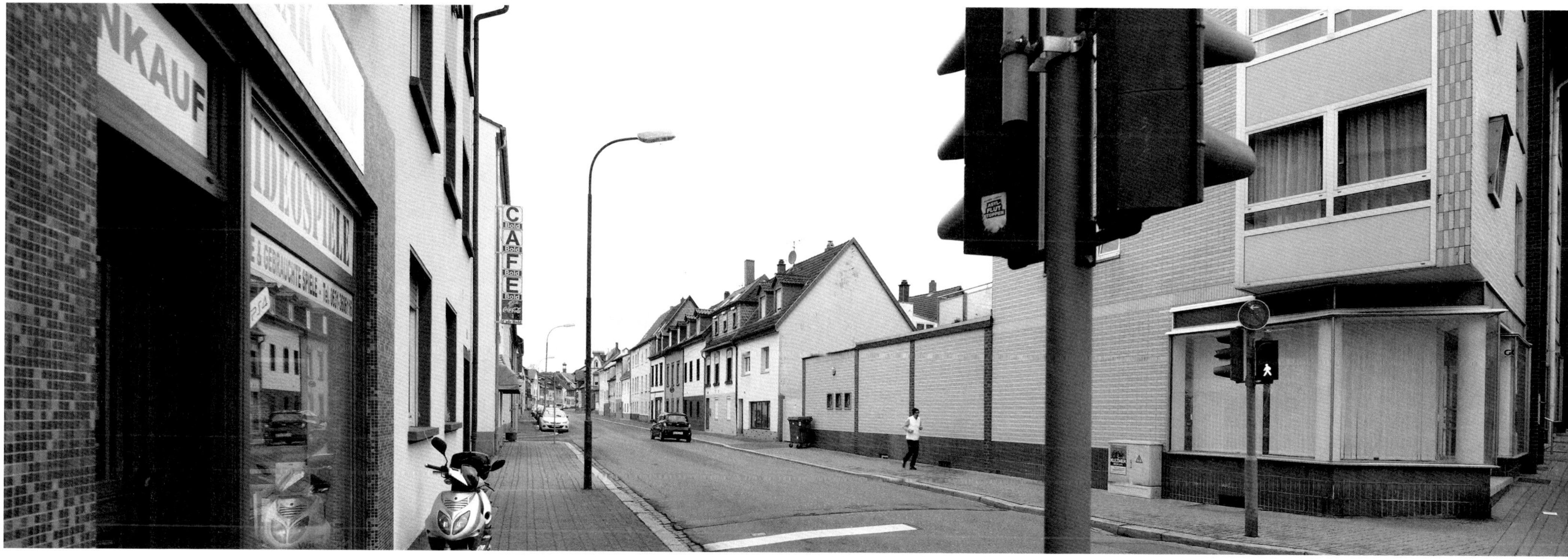

Kaiserslautern 2017

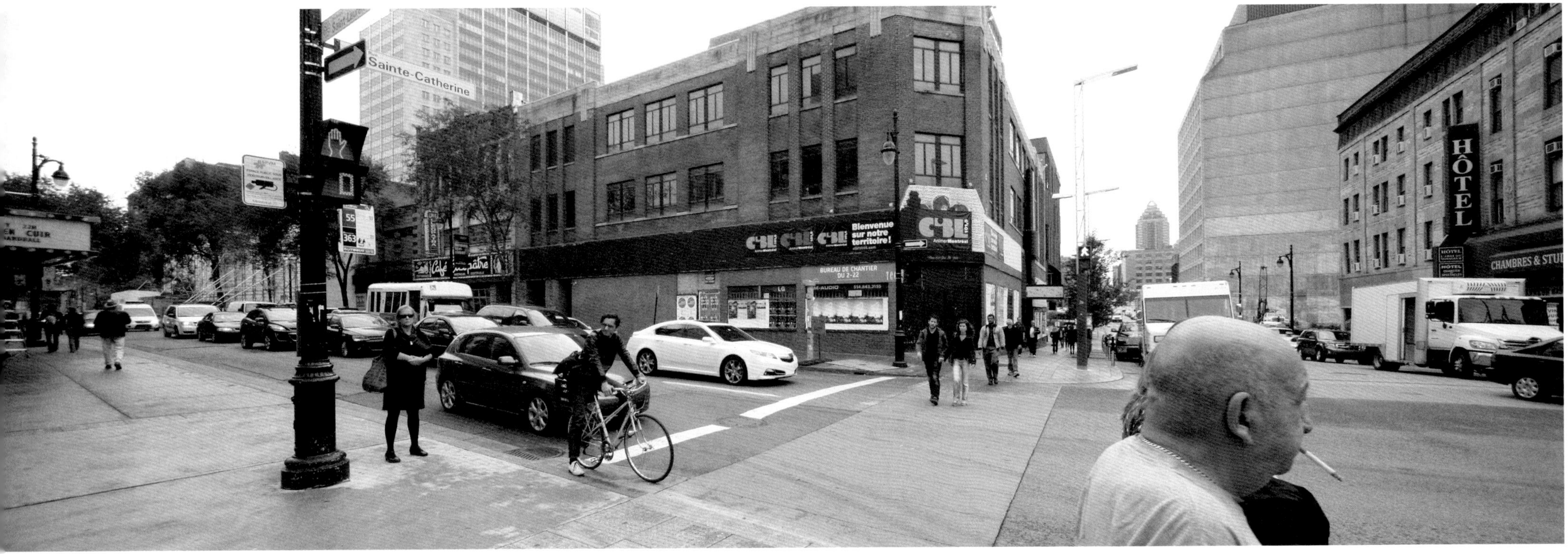

Montreal 2012

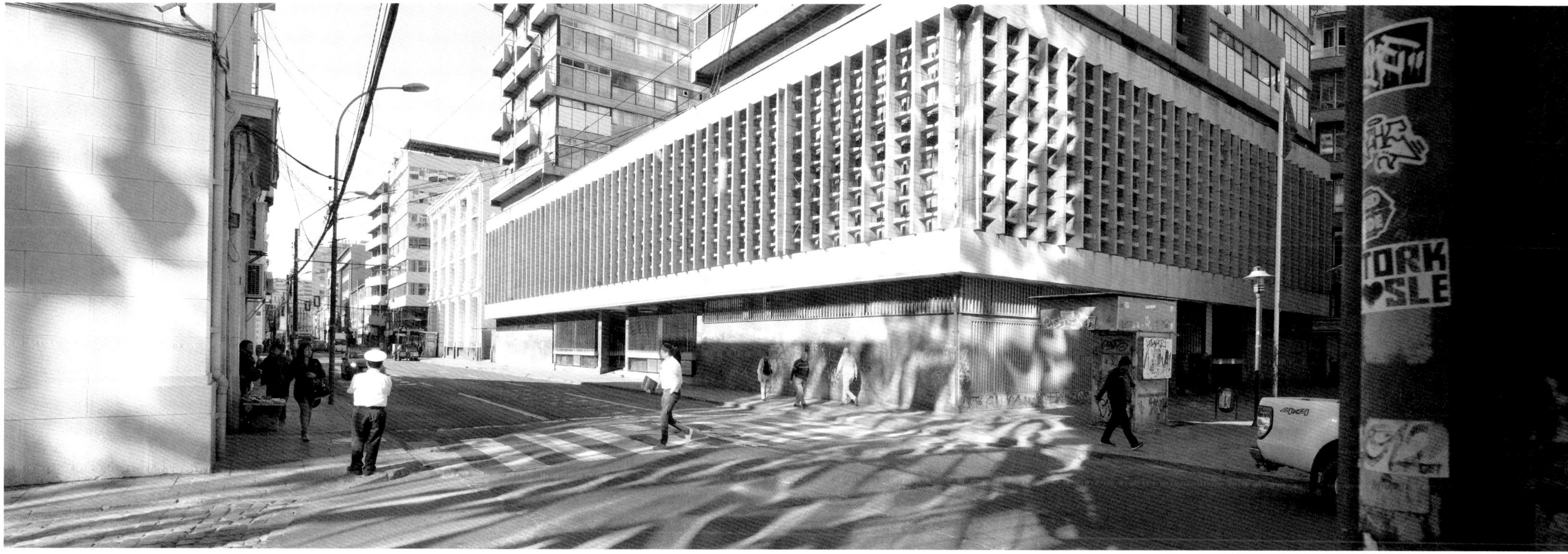

Valparaiso 2018

> Kanchipuram 2008

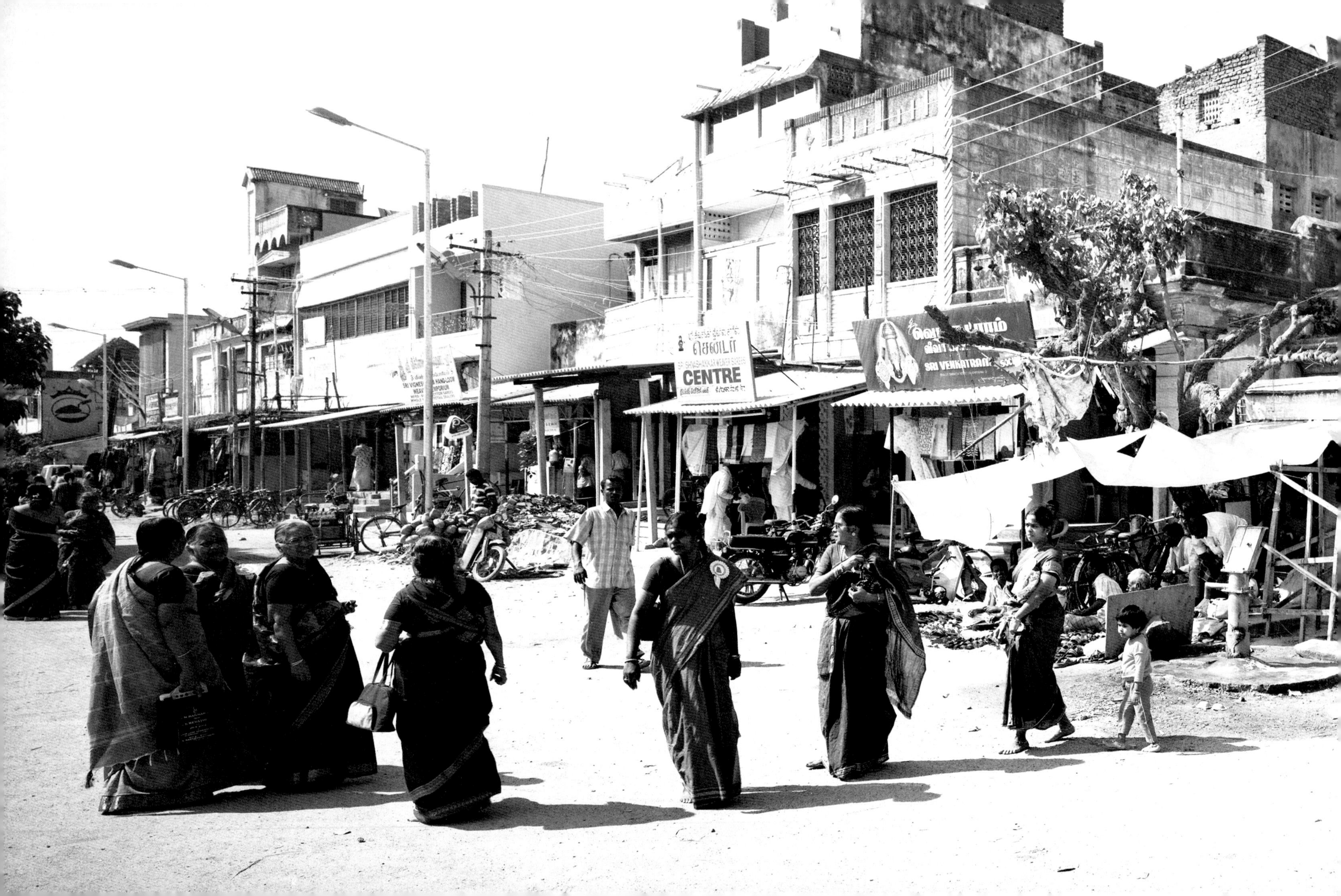
சென்டர்
SRI SHIVASHANKAR WEAVER SAREES
CENTRE

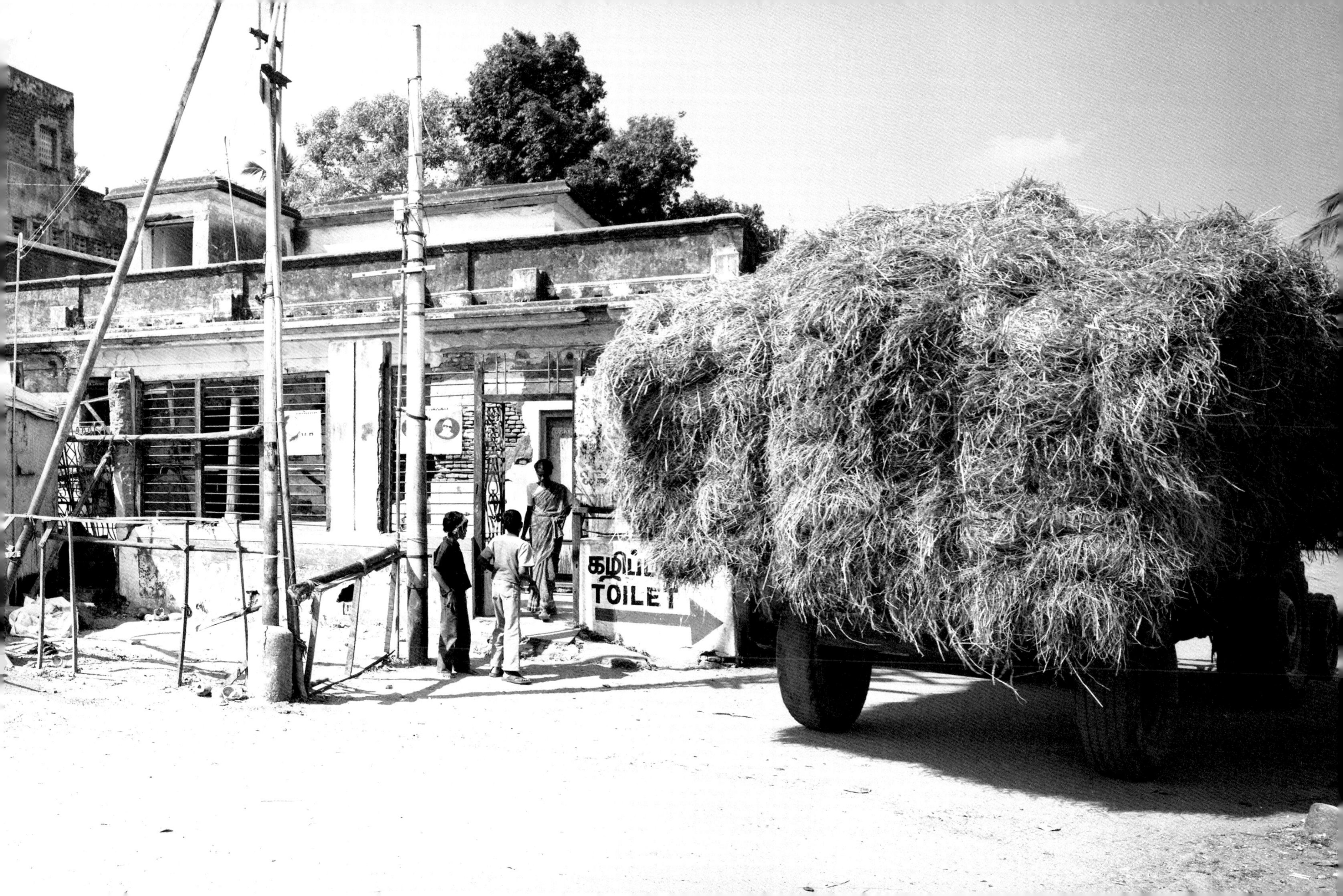
TOILET

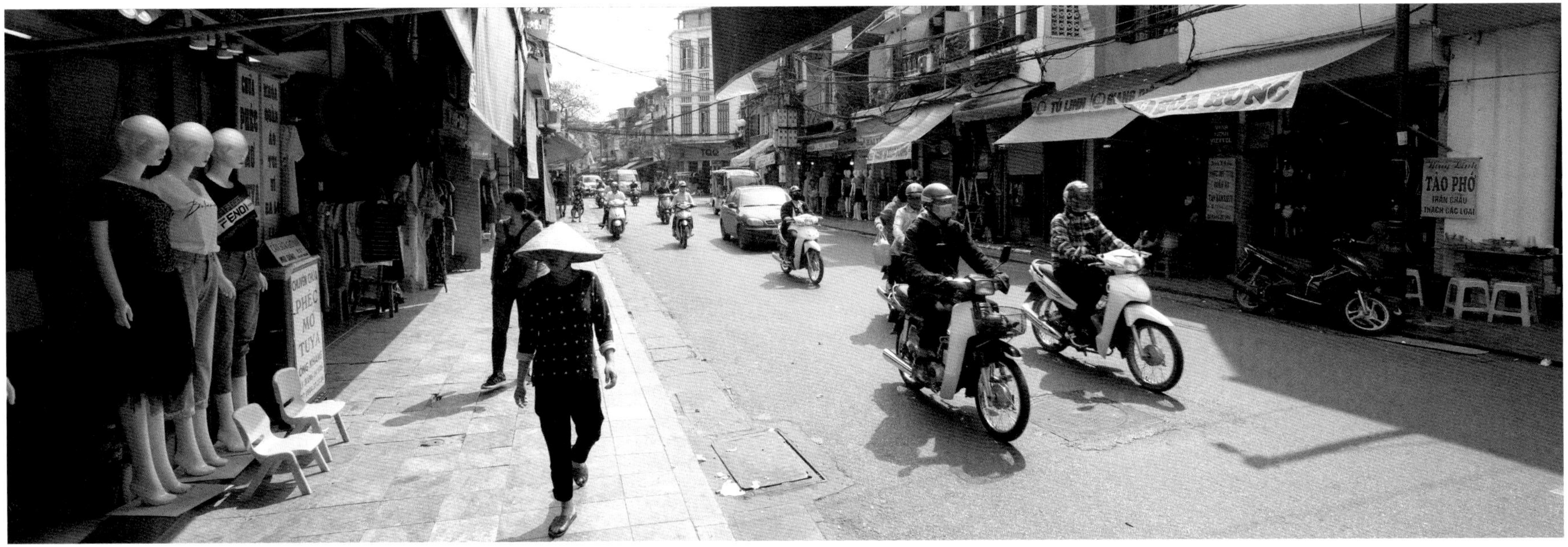
TÀO PHỚ

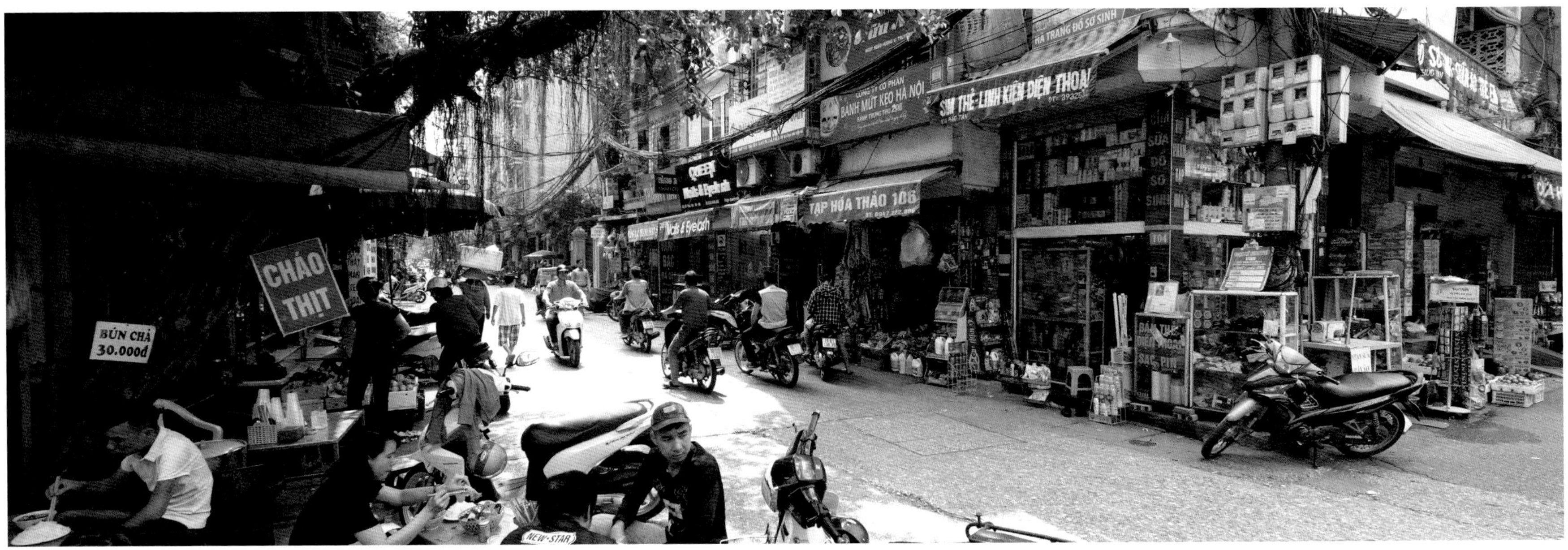
CHÁO THỊT
BÚN CHẢ 30.000đ
BÁNH MỨT KẸO HÀ NỘI
SIM THẺ- LINH KIỆN ĐIỆN THOẠI
TẠP HÓA THẢO 106

Hanoi 2019

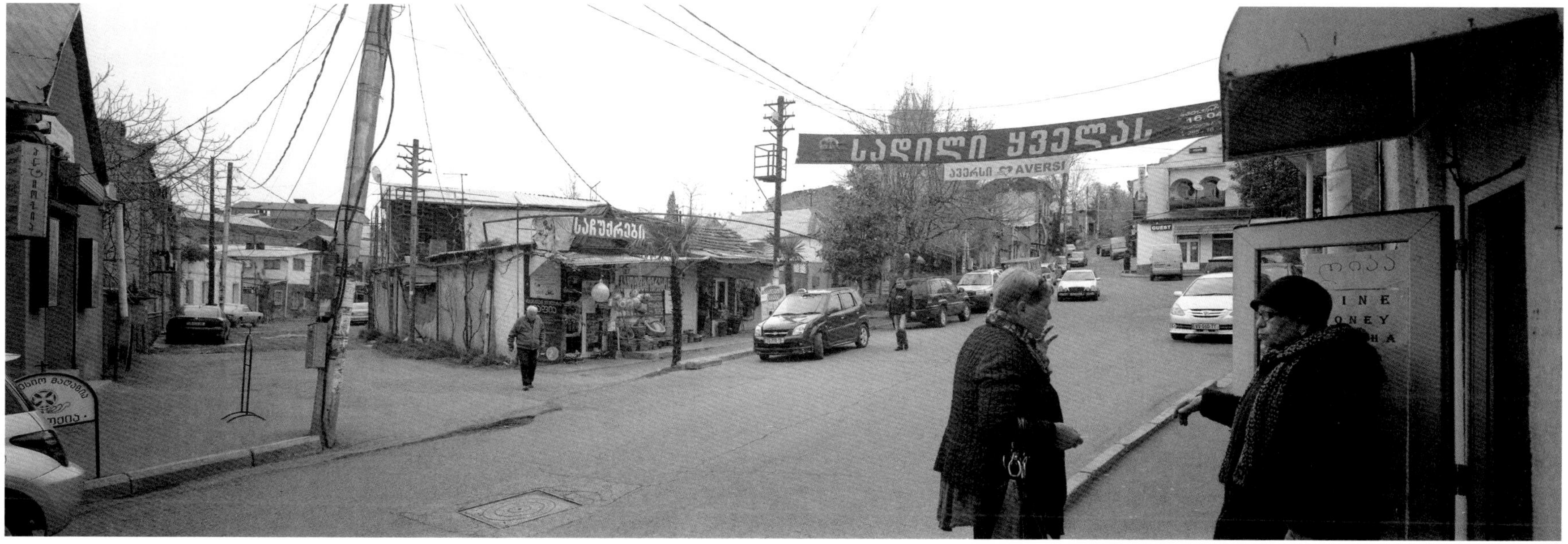
AVERSI

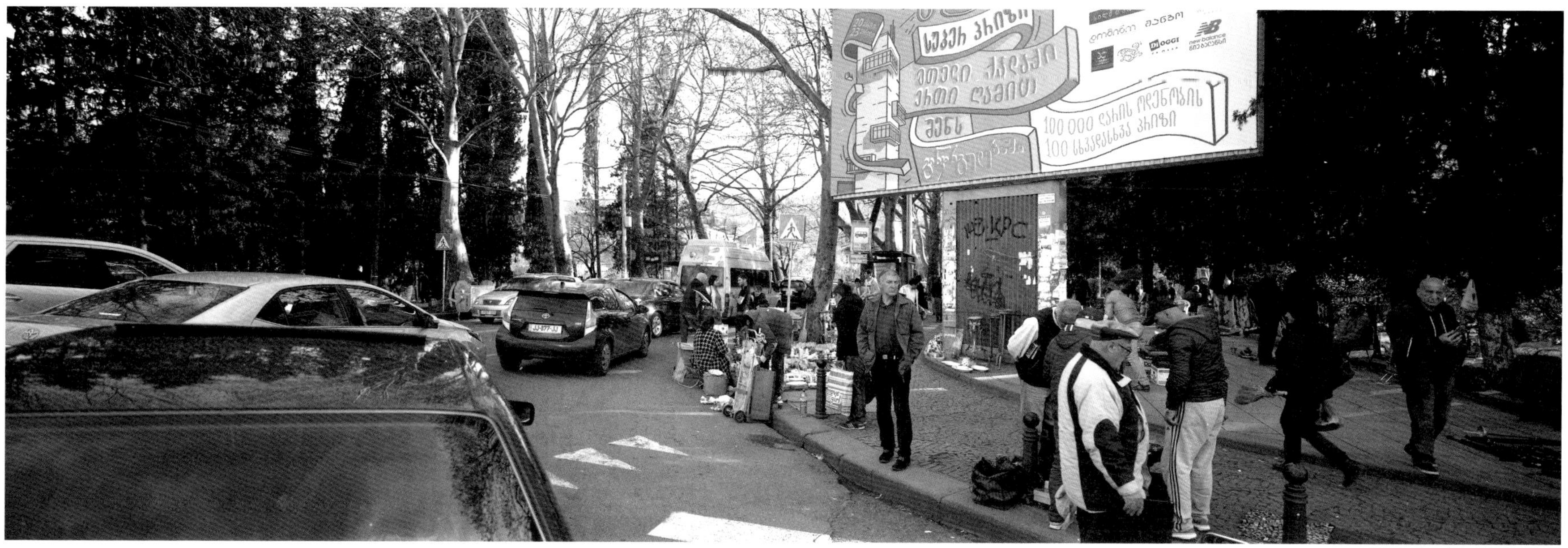
new balance

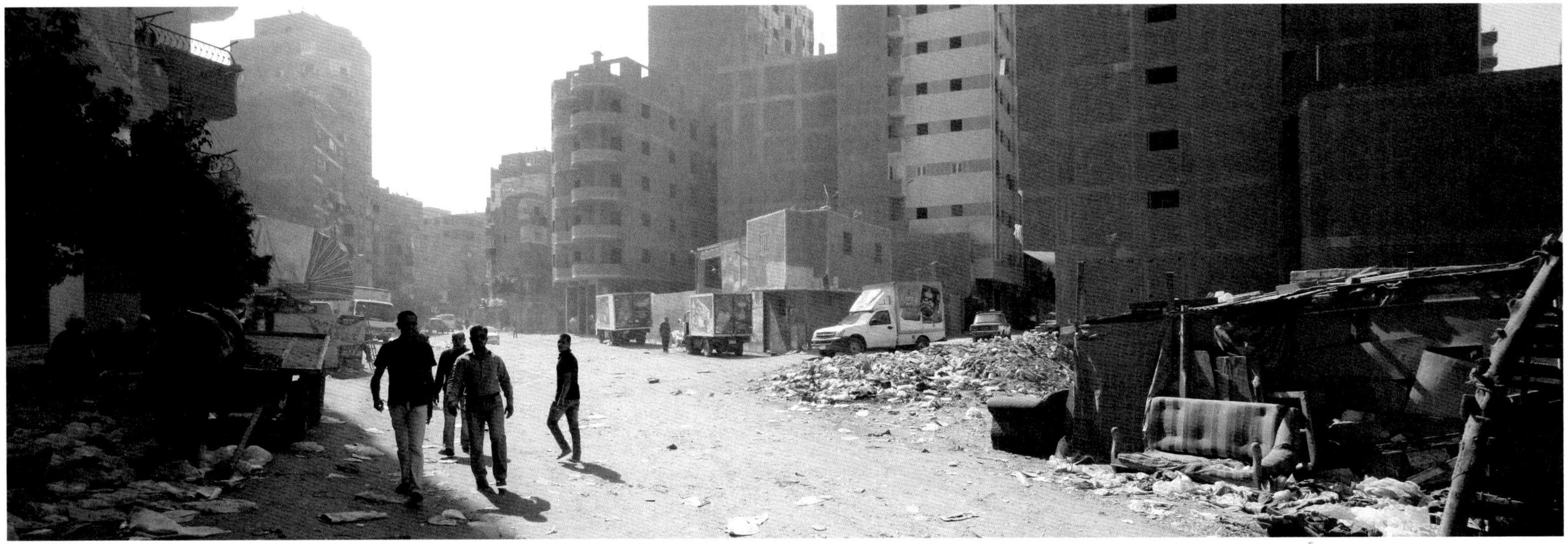

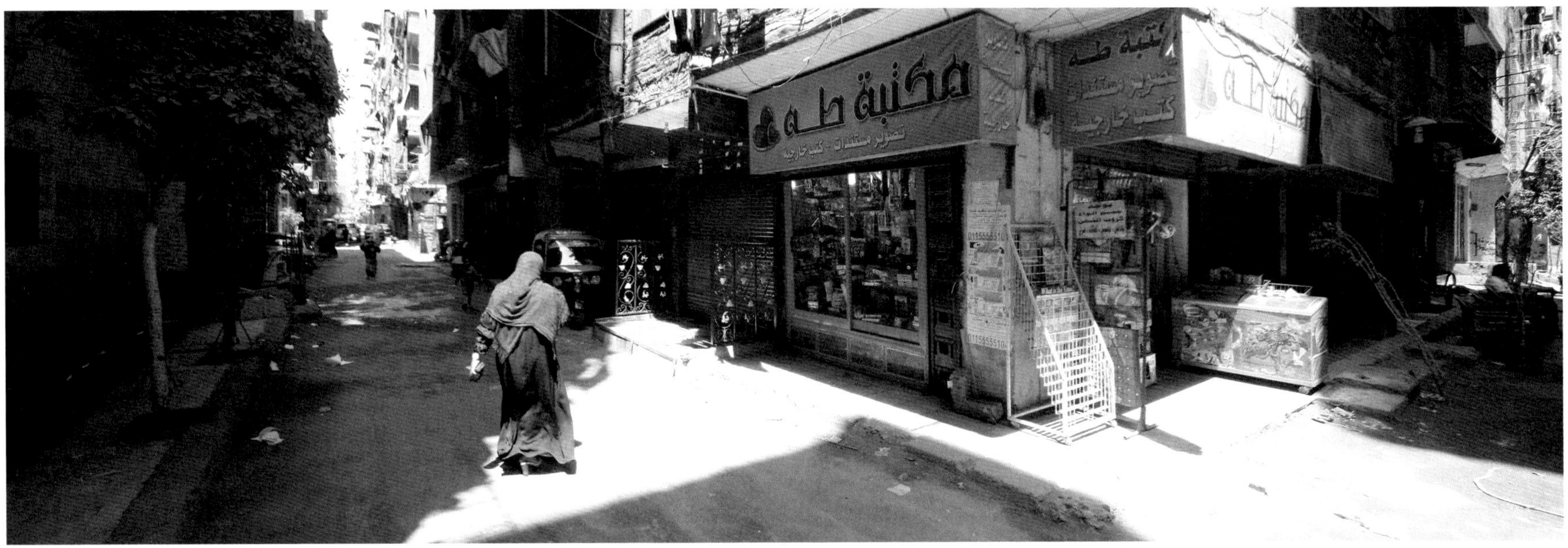

Cairo 2013

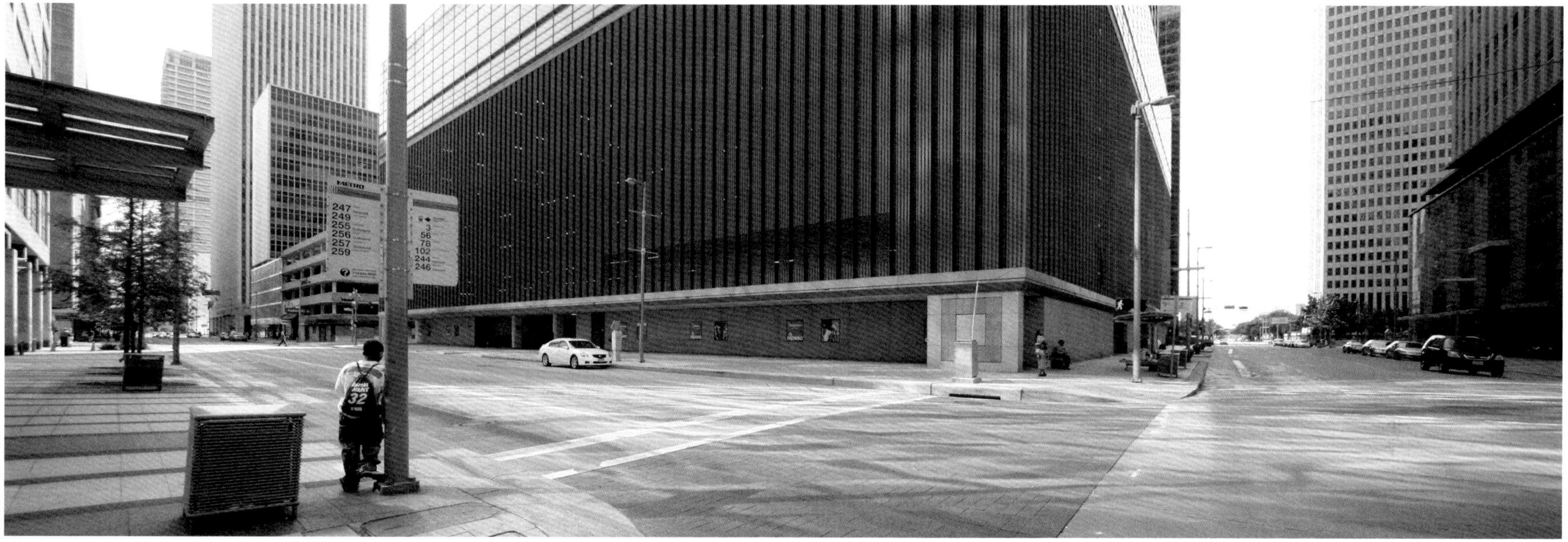

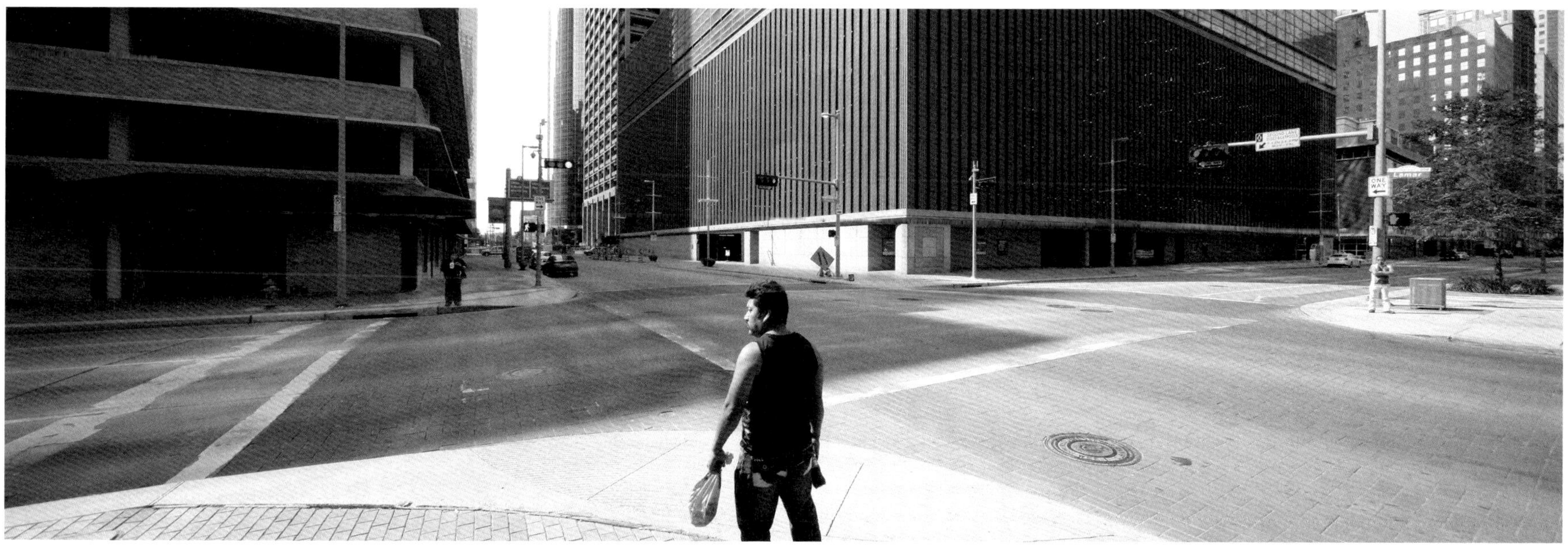

Houston 2011

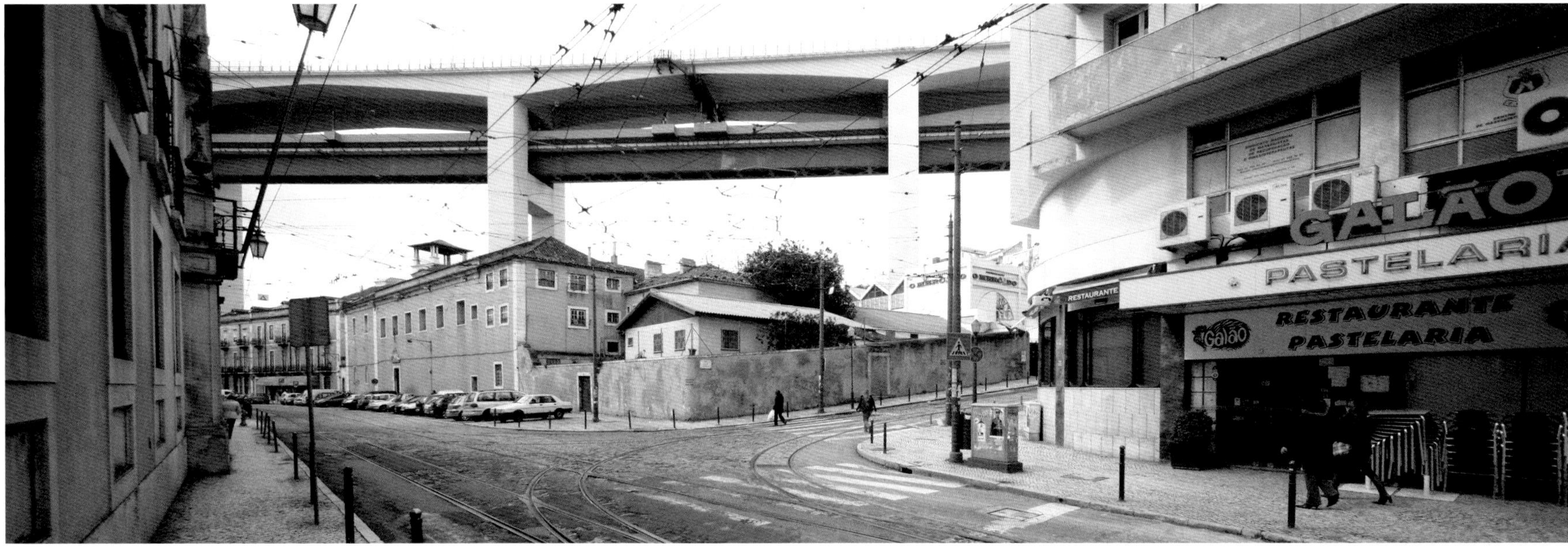
GALÃO
PASTELARIA
RESTAURANTE
RESTAURANTE
PASTELARIA

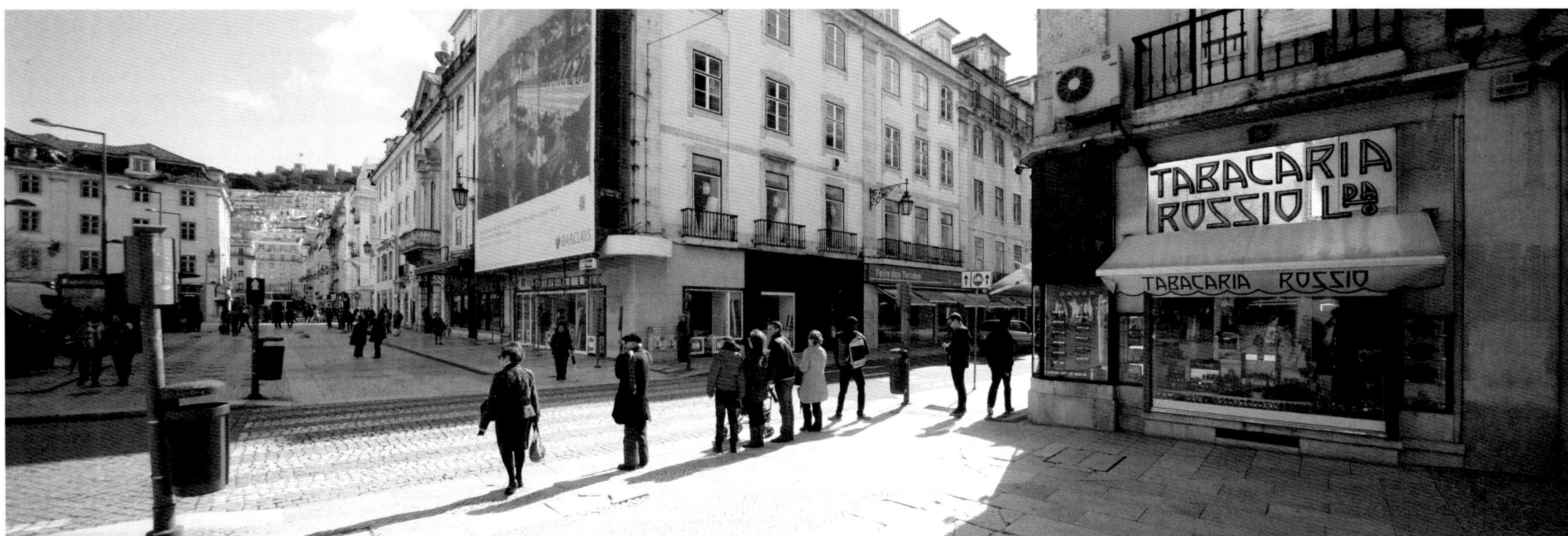
TABACARIA
ROSSIO Lda
TABACARIA ROSSIO

Lisboa 2014

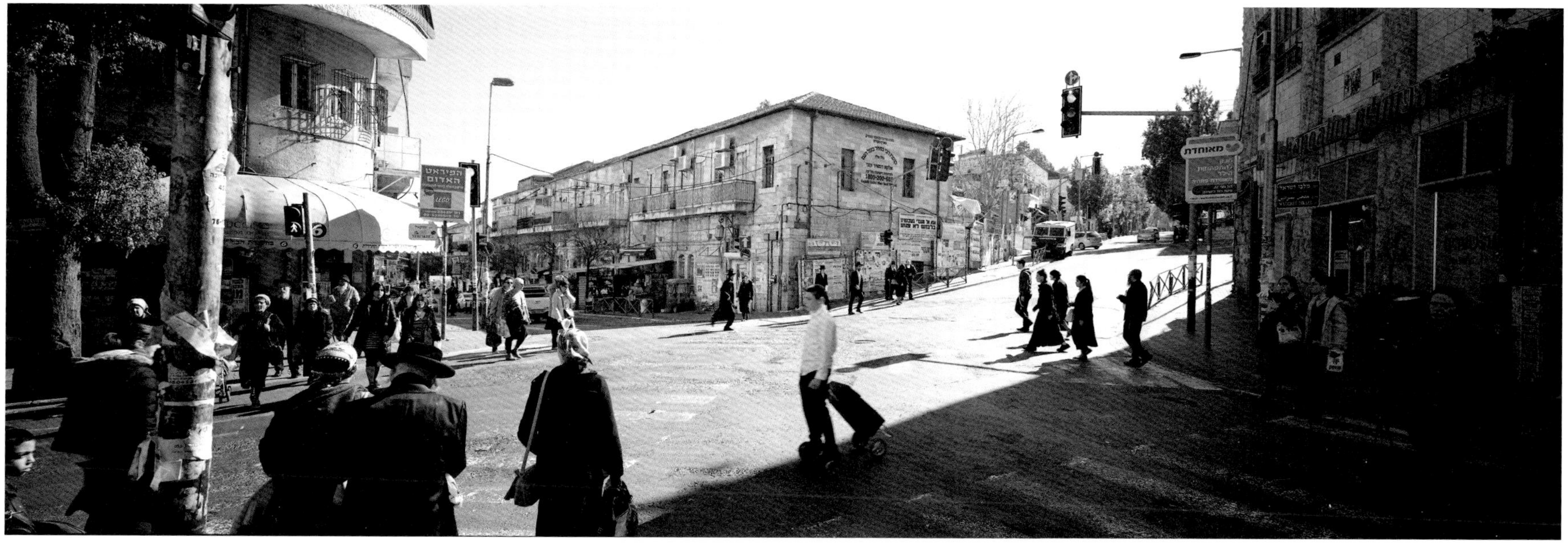

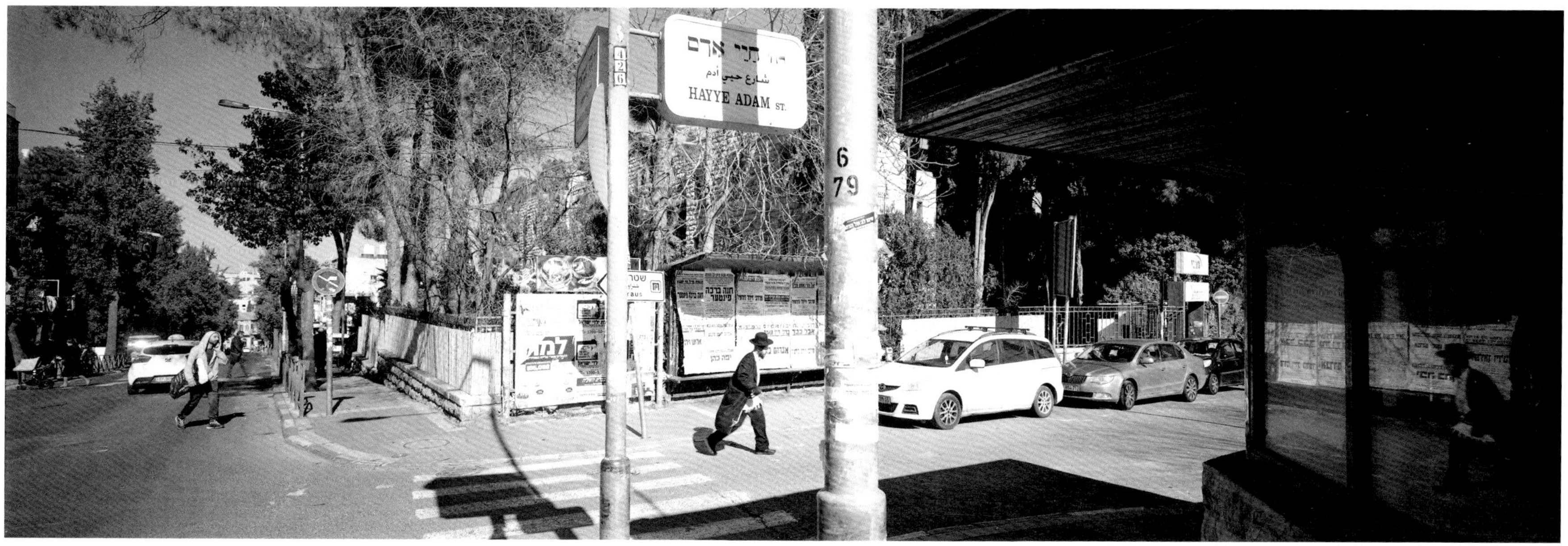
HAYYE ADAM ST.

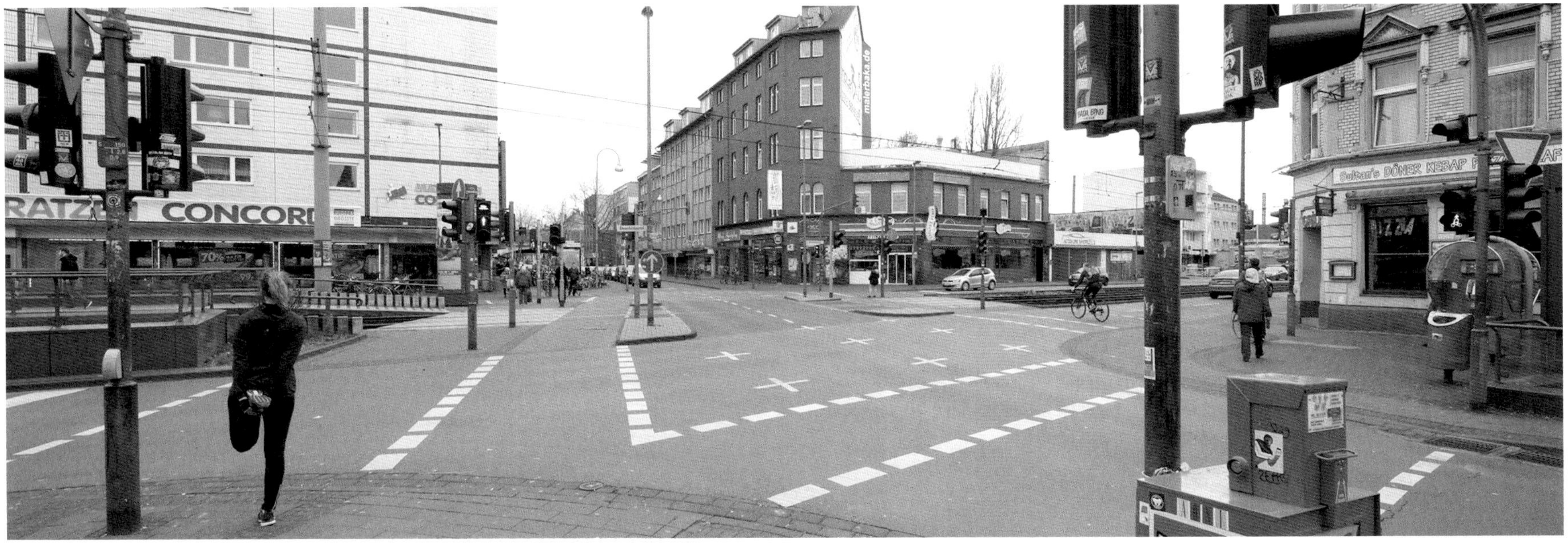

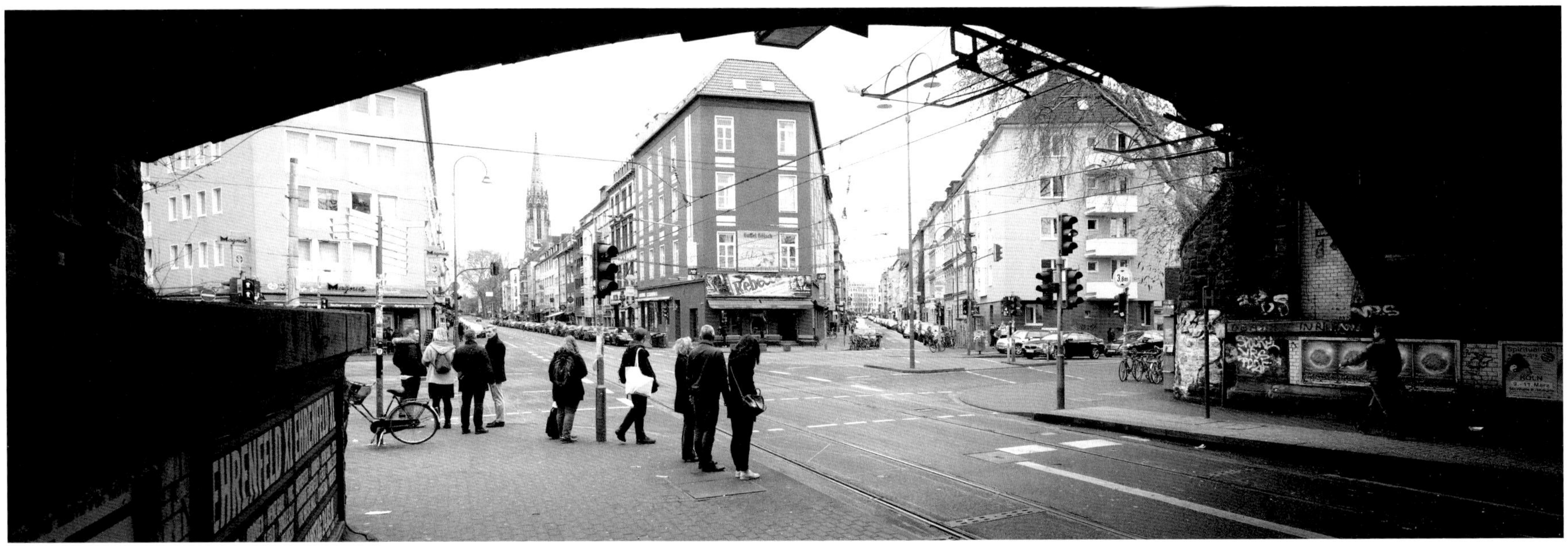

Köln 2018

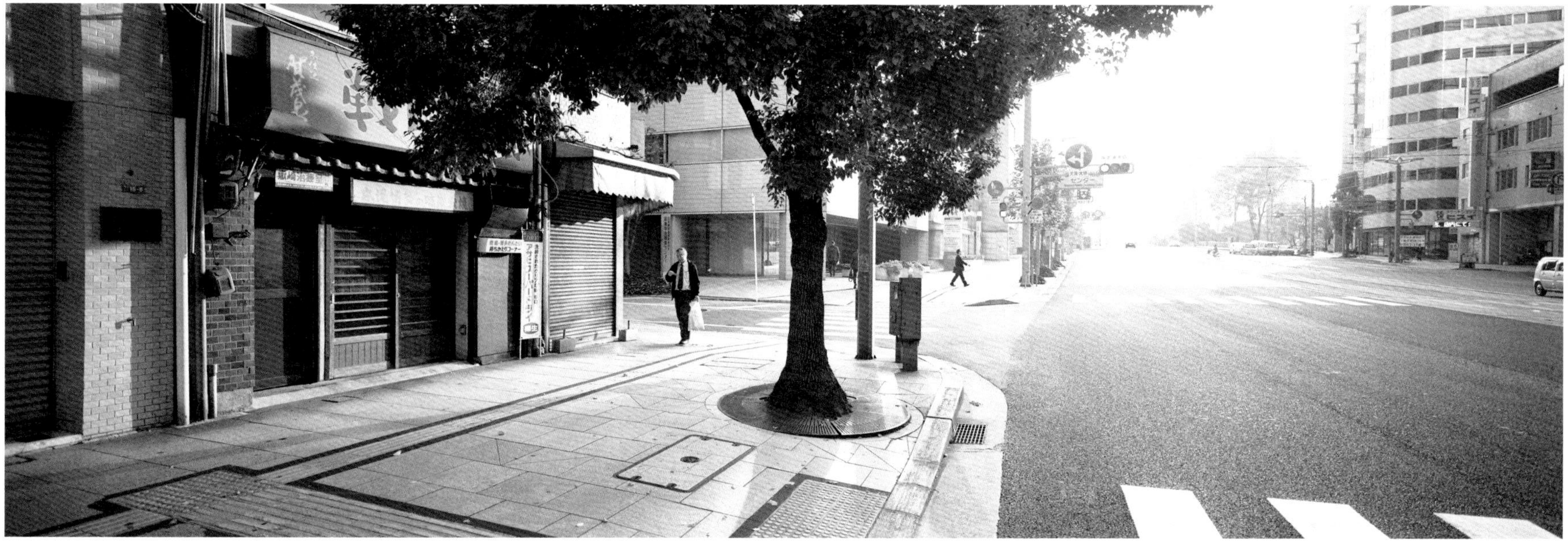

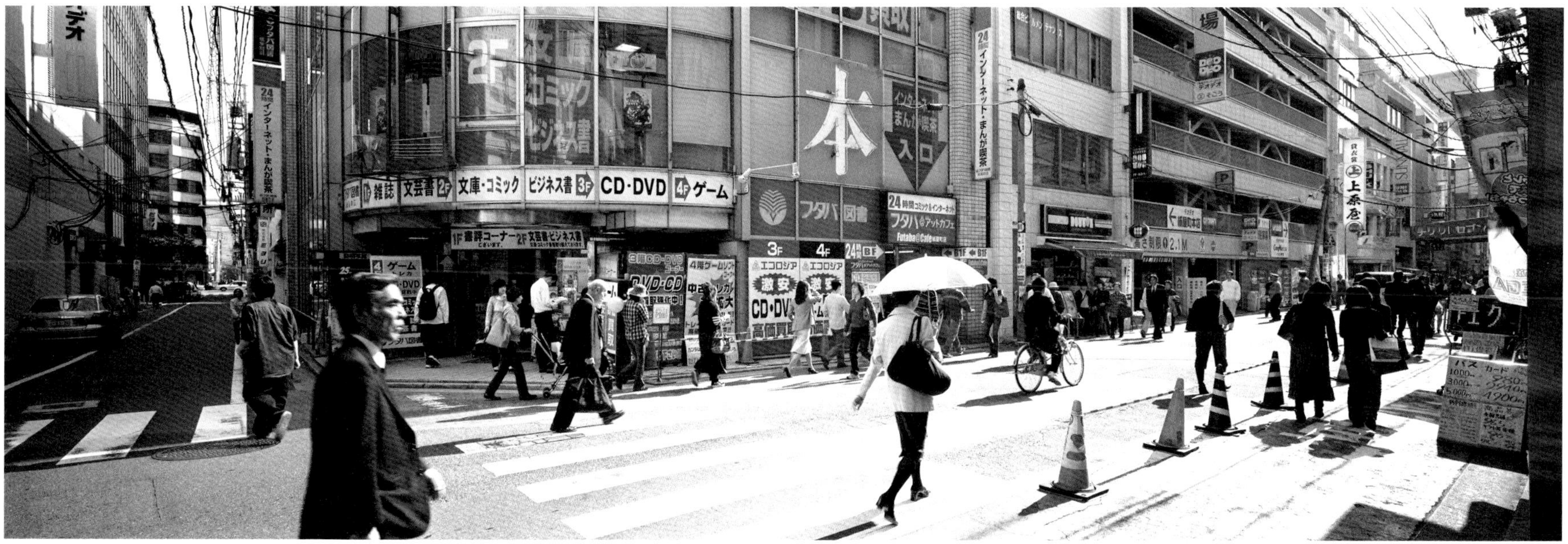

Hiroshima 2005

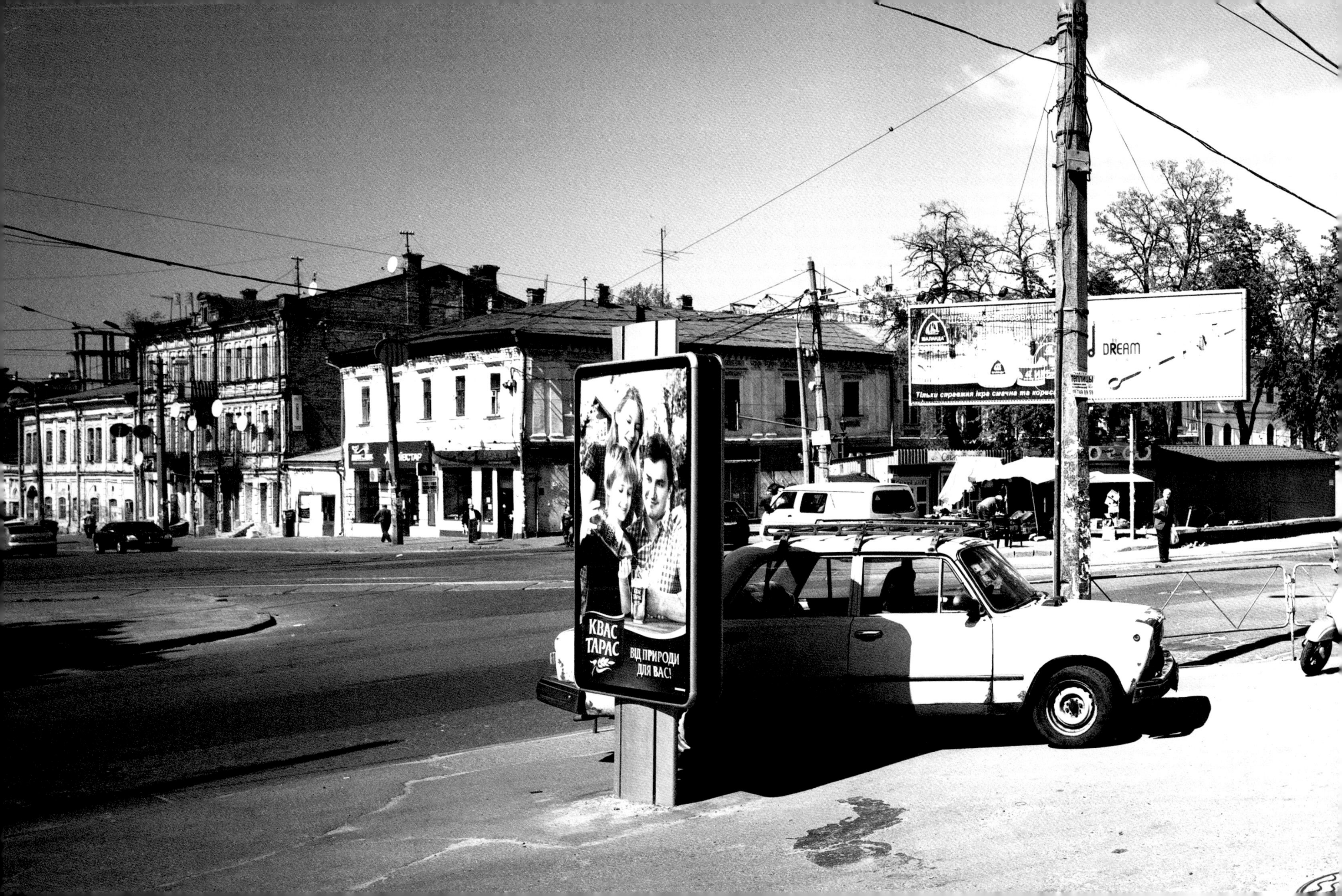
КВАС
ТАРАС
ВІД ПРИРОДИ
ДЛЯ ВАС!
DREAM

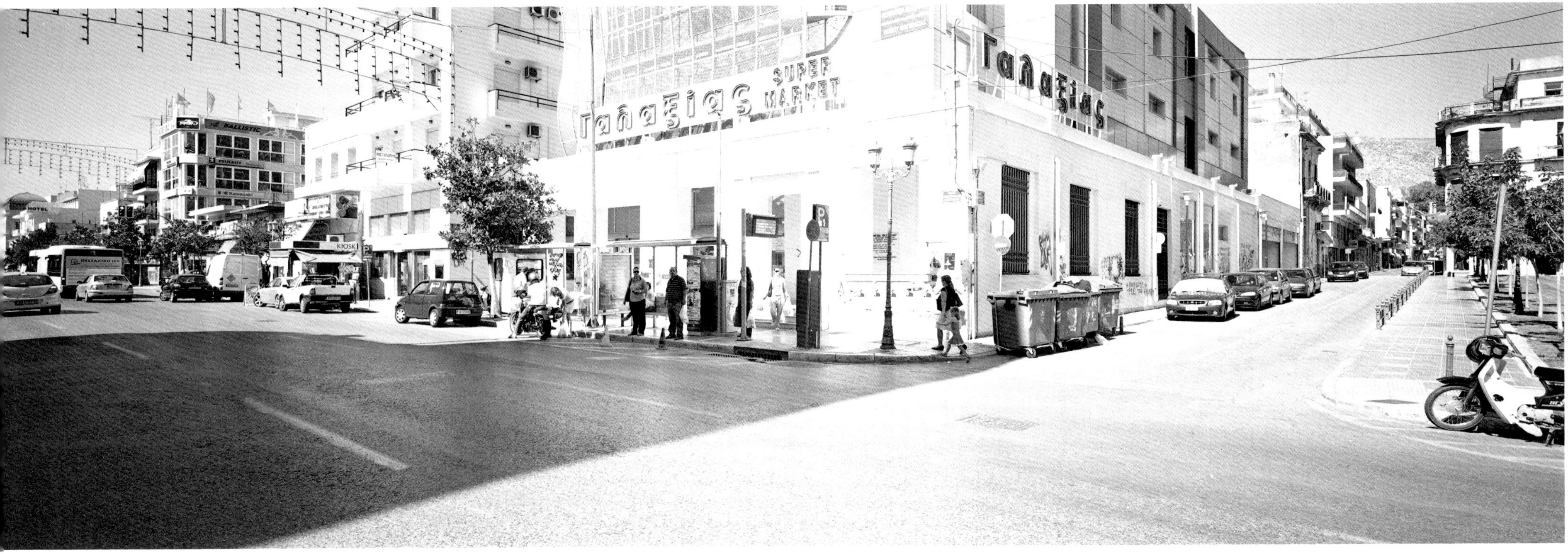

Volos 2010

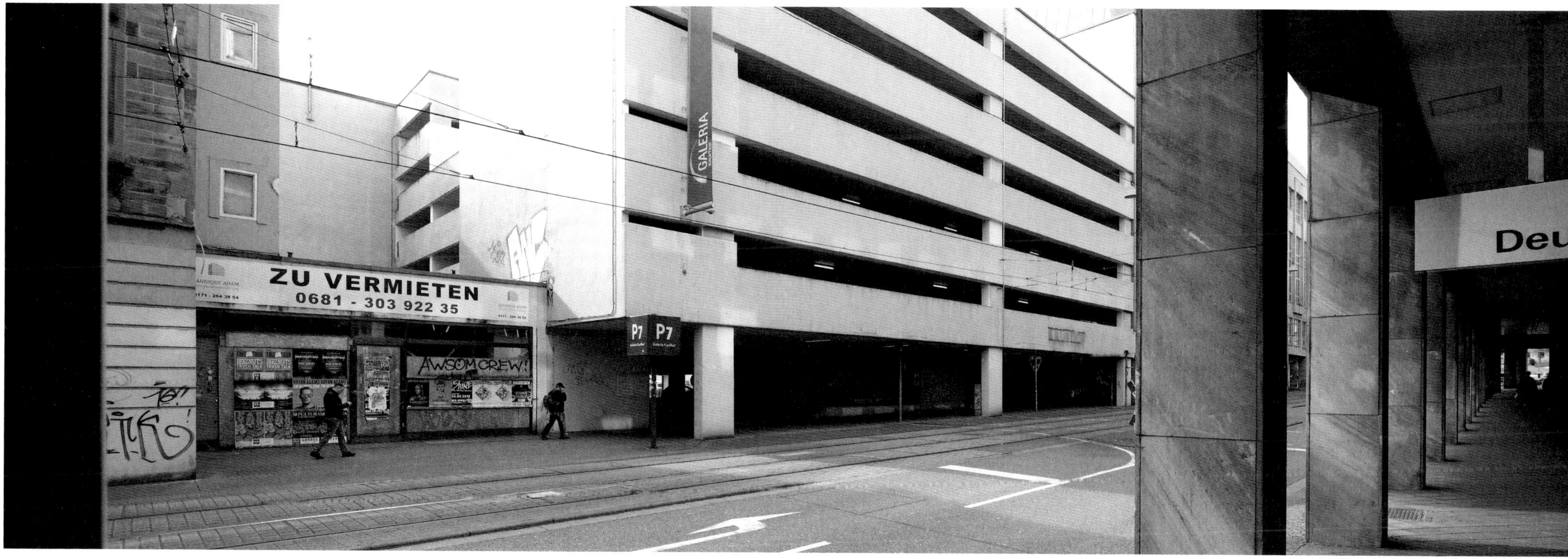

Saarbrücken 2016

< Kiew 2010

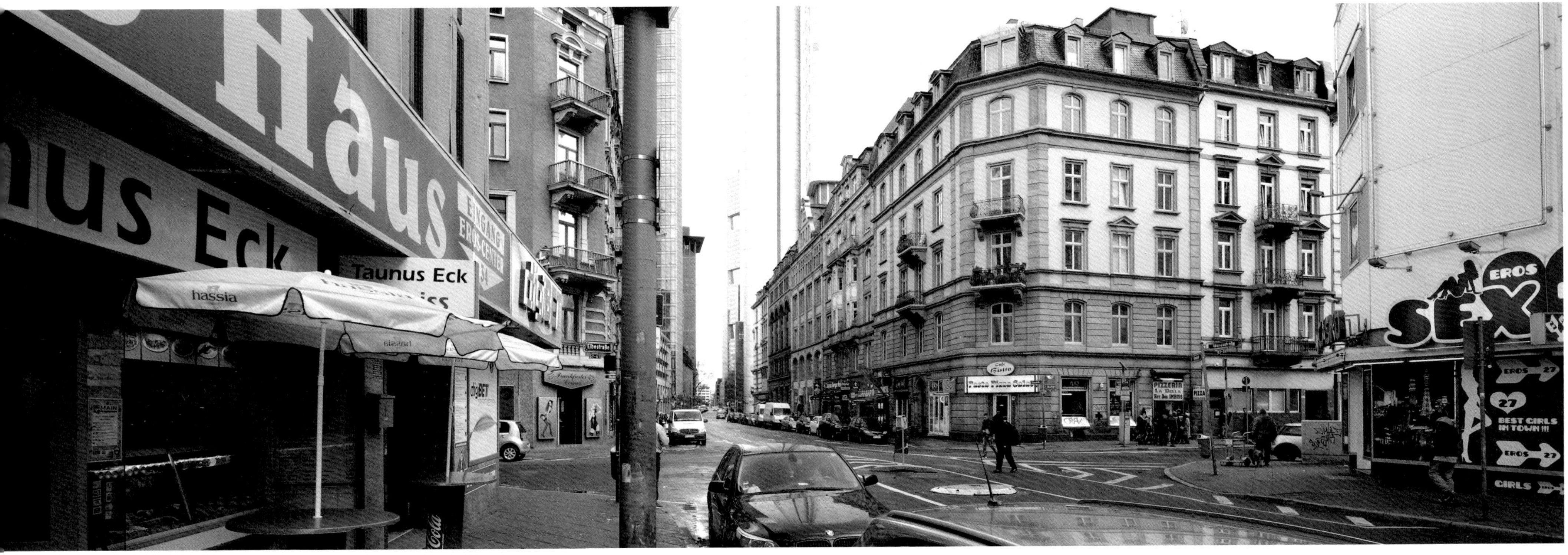

Frankfurt 2015

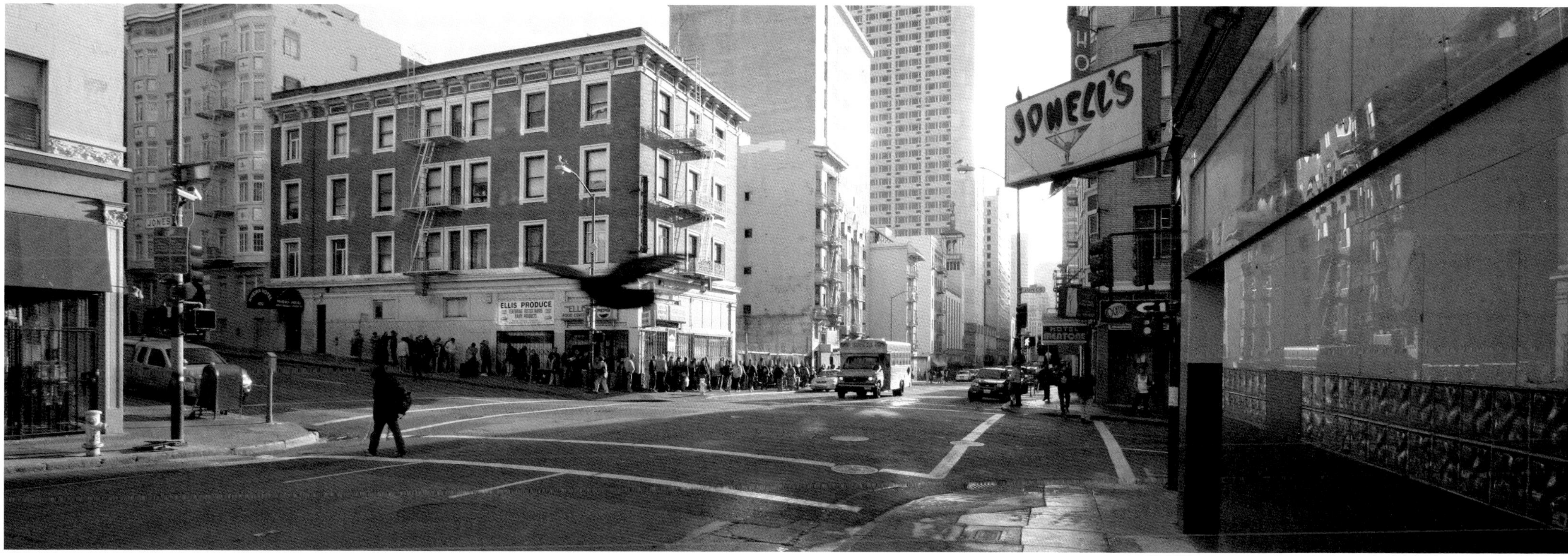

San Francisco 2009

> Cairo 2003

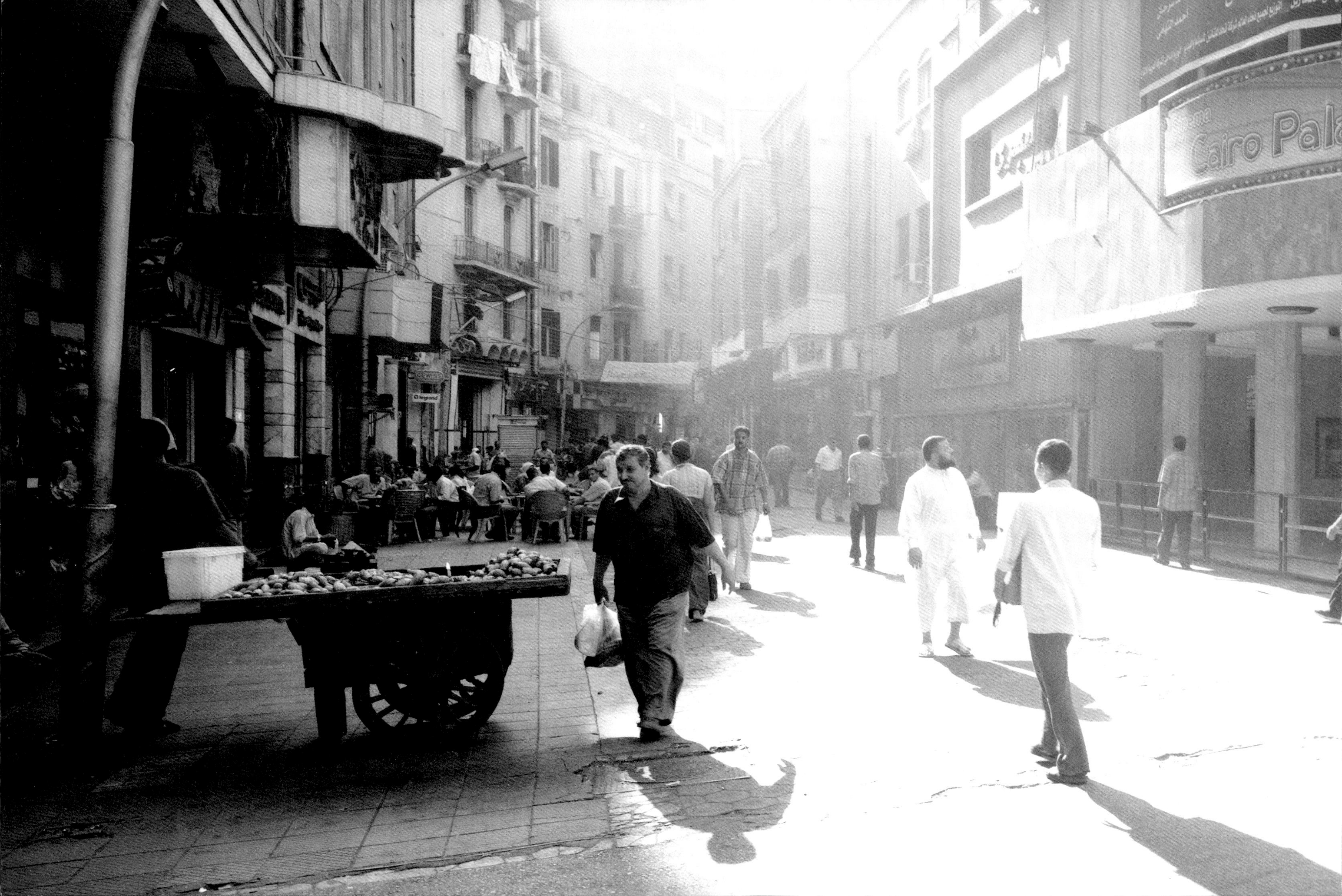
Cairo Pala

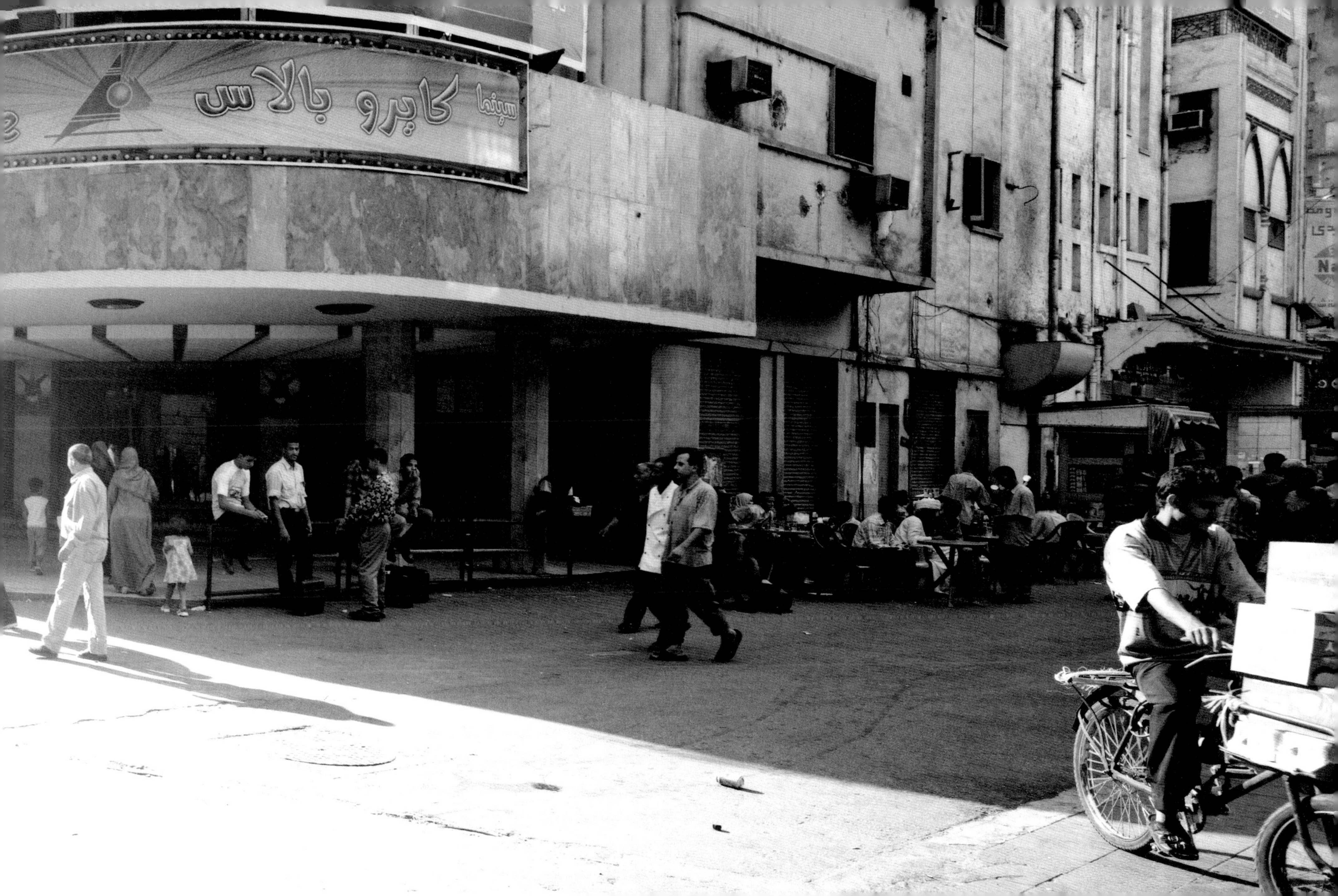
سينما كايرو بالاس

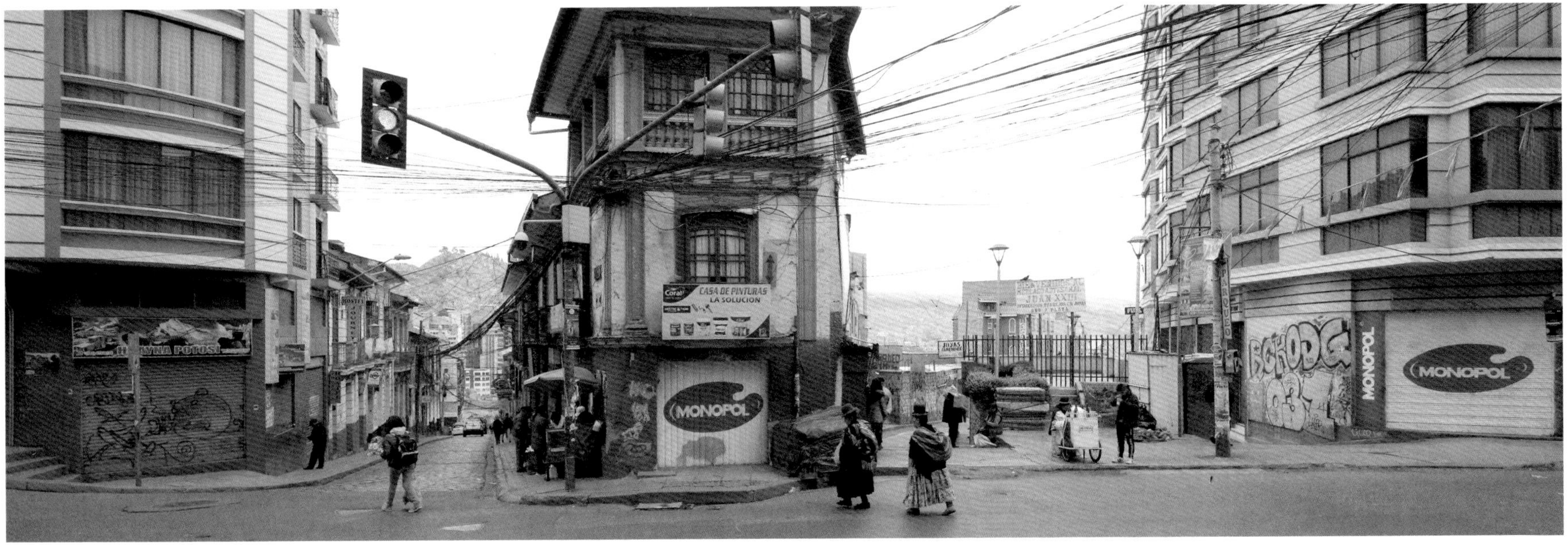
CASA DE PINTURAS
LA SOLUCION
MONOPOL
MONOPOL
MONOPOL

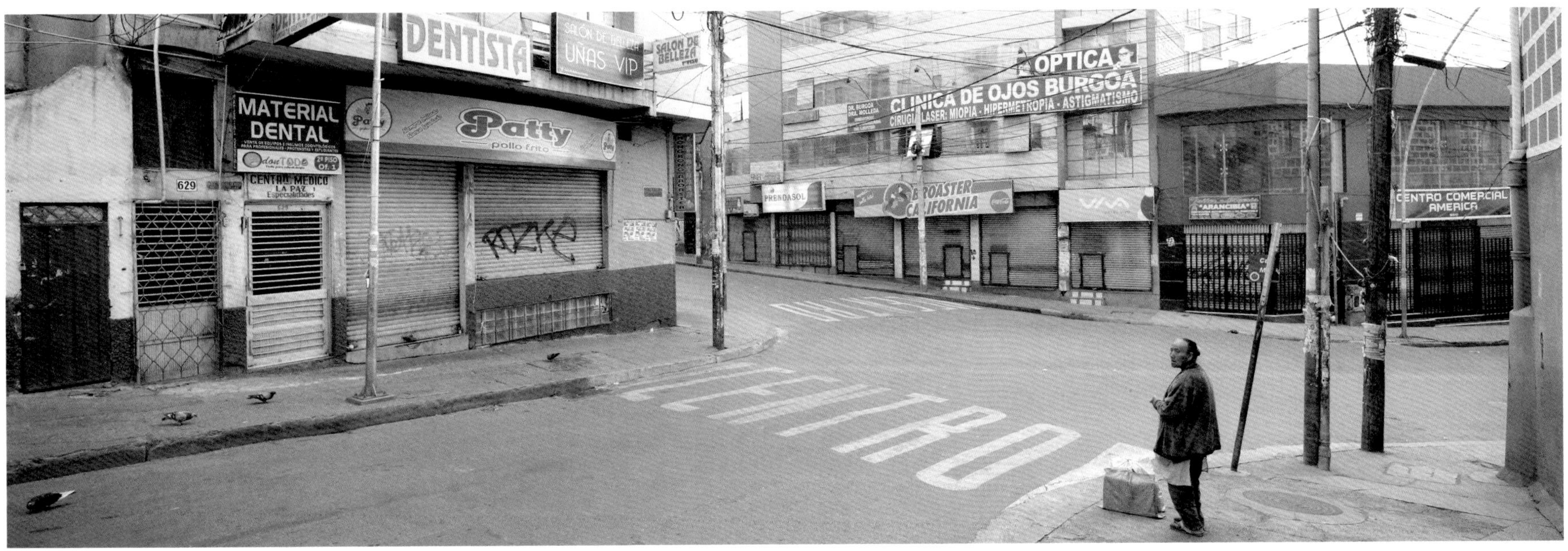
DENTISTA
SALON DE BELLEZA
UÑAS VIP
SALON DE BELLEZA
MATERIAL DENTAL
Patty
pollo frito
629
CENTRO MEDICO
LA PAZ
Especialidades
OPTICA
CLINICA DE OJOS BURGOA
CIRUGIA LASER: MIOPIA - HIPERMETROPIA - ASTIGMATISMO
PRENDASOL
BROASTER
CALIFORNIA
"ARANCIBIA"
CENTRO COMERCIAL
AMERICA
CENTRO

La Paz 2018

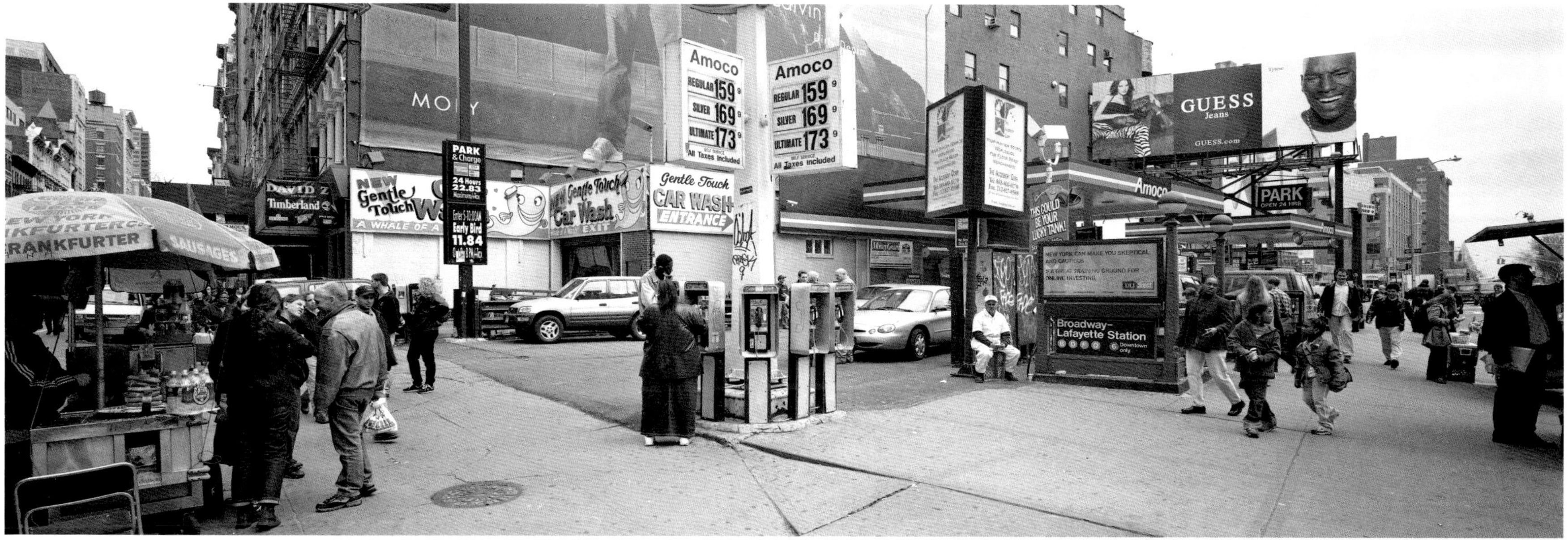
Amoco
REGULAR 159
SILVER 169
ULTIMATE 173
All Taxes Included
GUESS
Jeans
GUESS.com
PARK & Charge
24 Hours 22.83
Early Bird 11.84
Gentle Touch
CAR WASH
ENTRANCE
Timberland
FRANKFURTER
SAUSAGES
Broadway–Lafayette Station
PARK

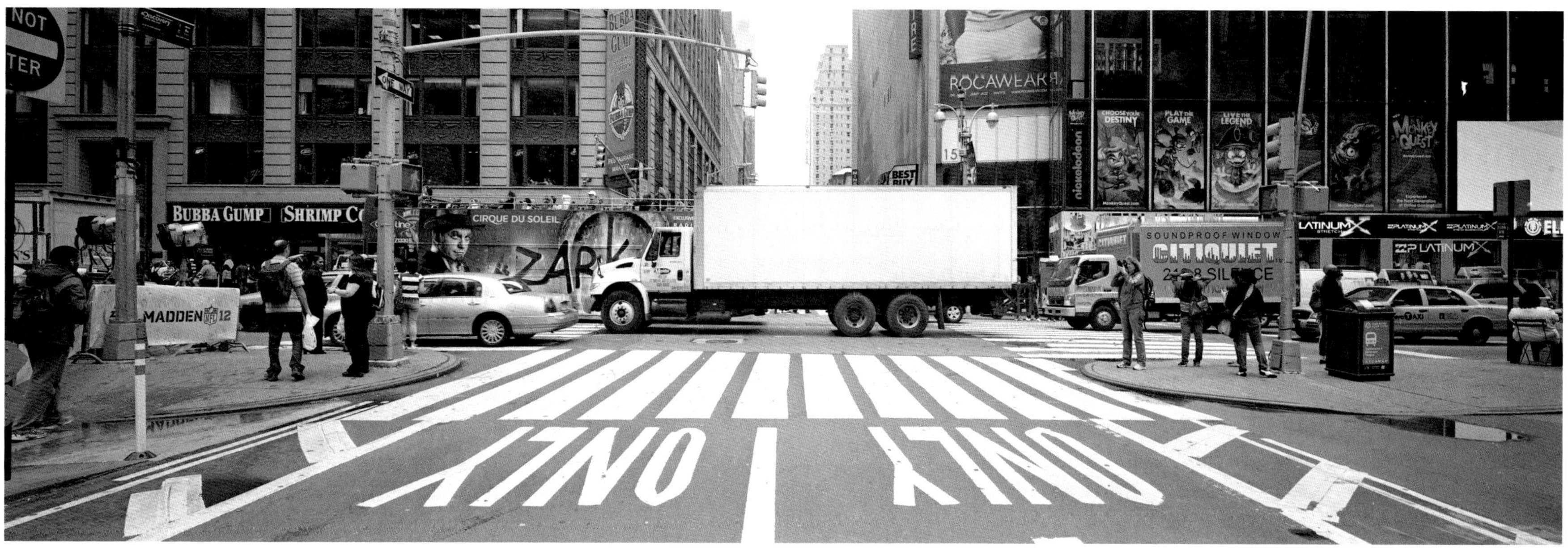
ONE WAY
BUBBA GUMP
SHRIMP CO
CIRQUE DU SOLEIL
ROCAWEAR
nickelodeon
MADDEN NFL 12
SOUNDPROOF WINDOW
CITIQUIET
ONLY
ONLY

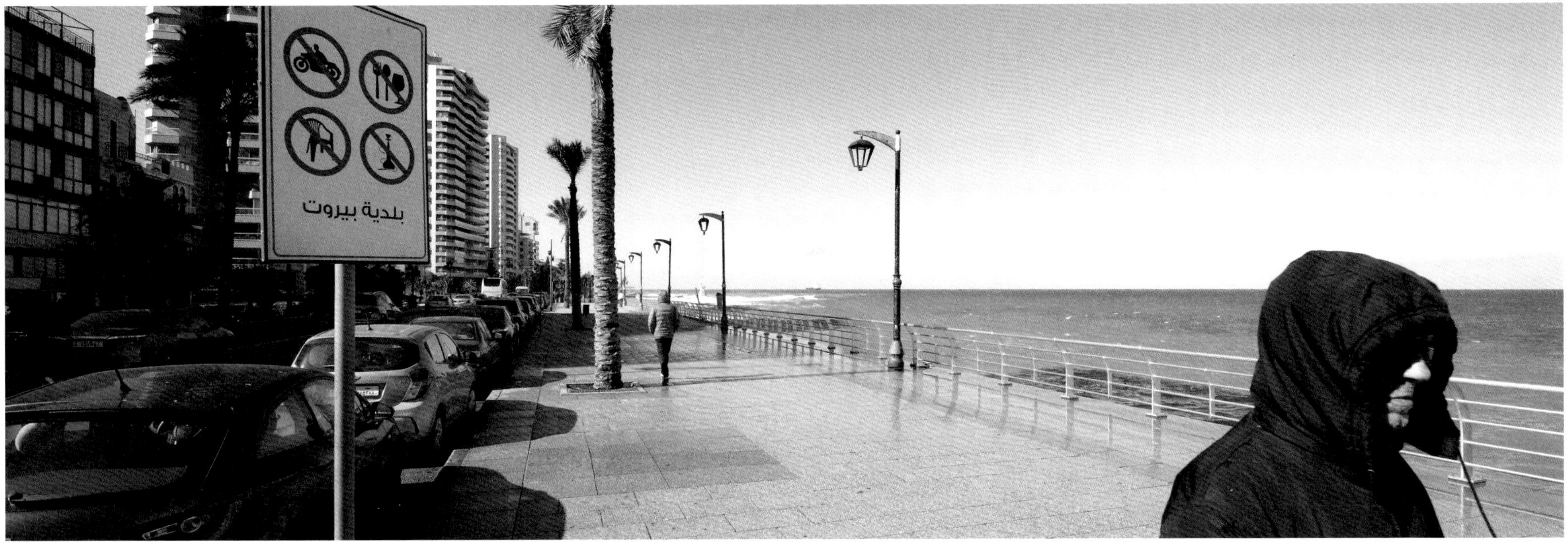
بلدية بيروت

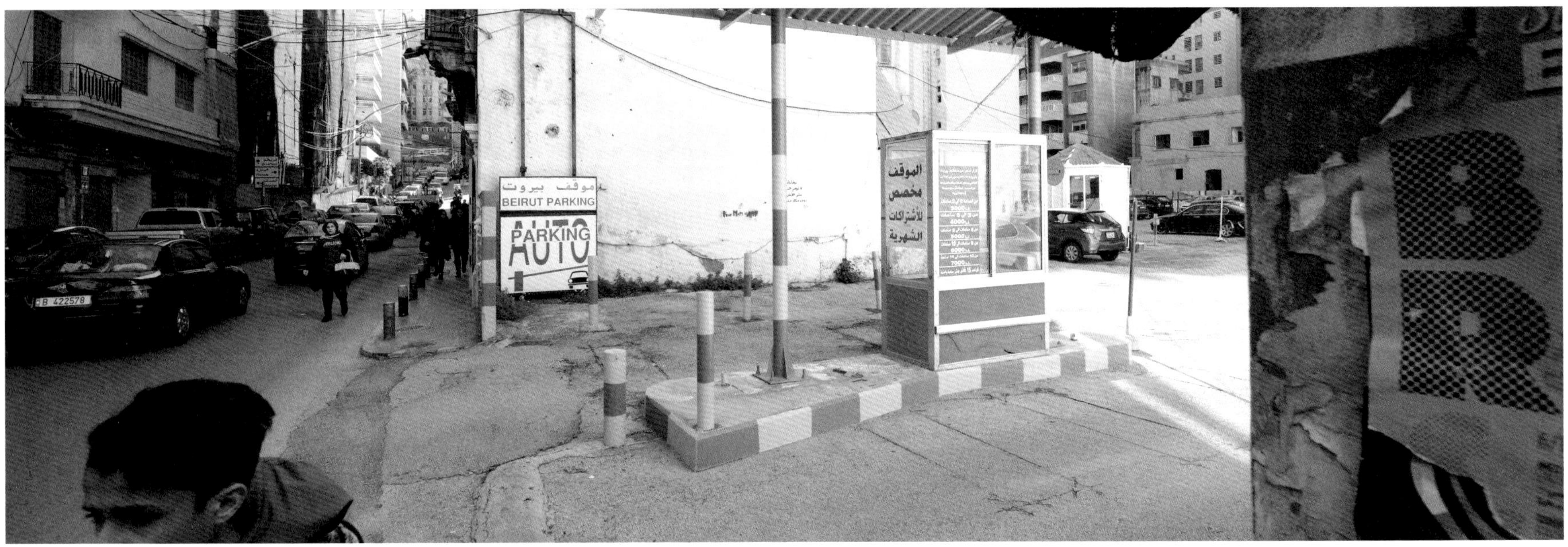
موقف بيروت
BEIRUT PARKING
AUTO
PARKING
الموقف
مخصص
للأشتراكات
الشهرية
B 422578

Beirut 2019

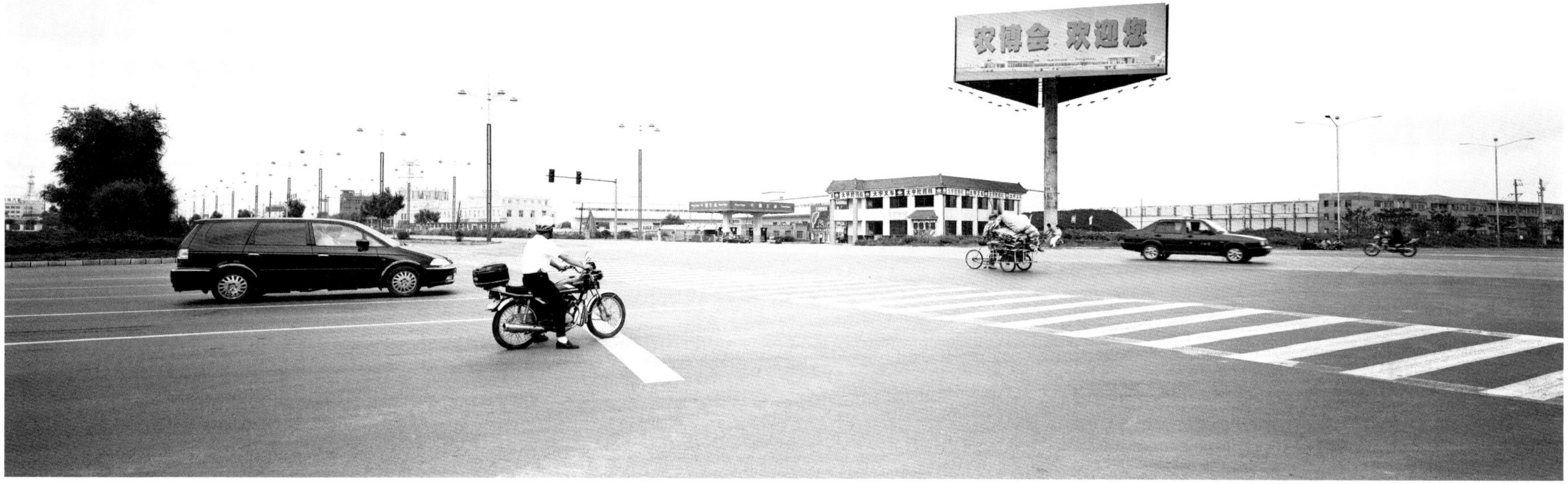

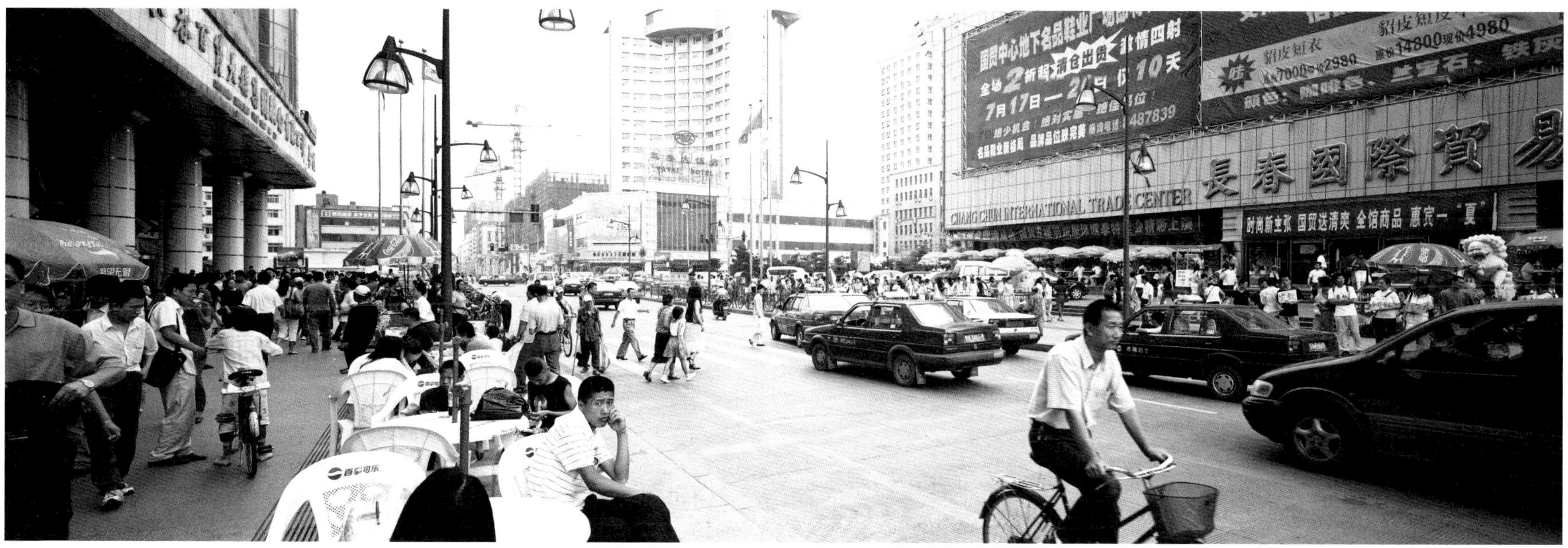

Changchun 2003

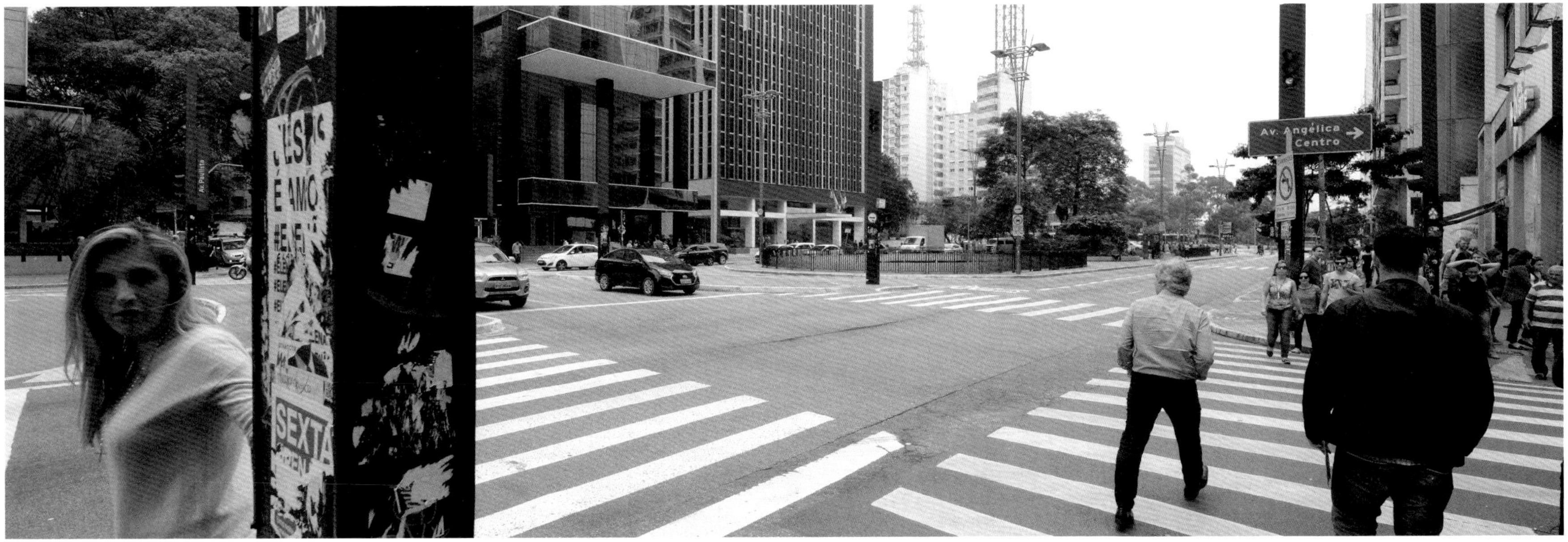

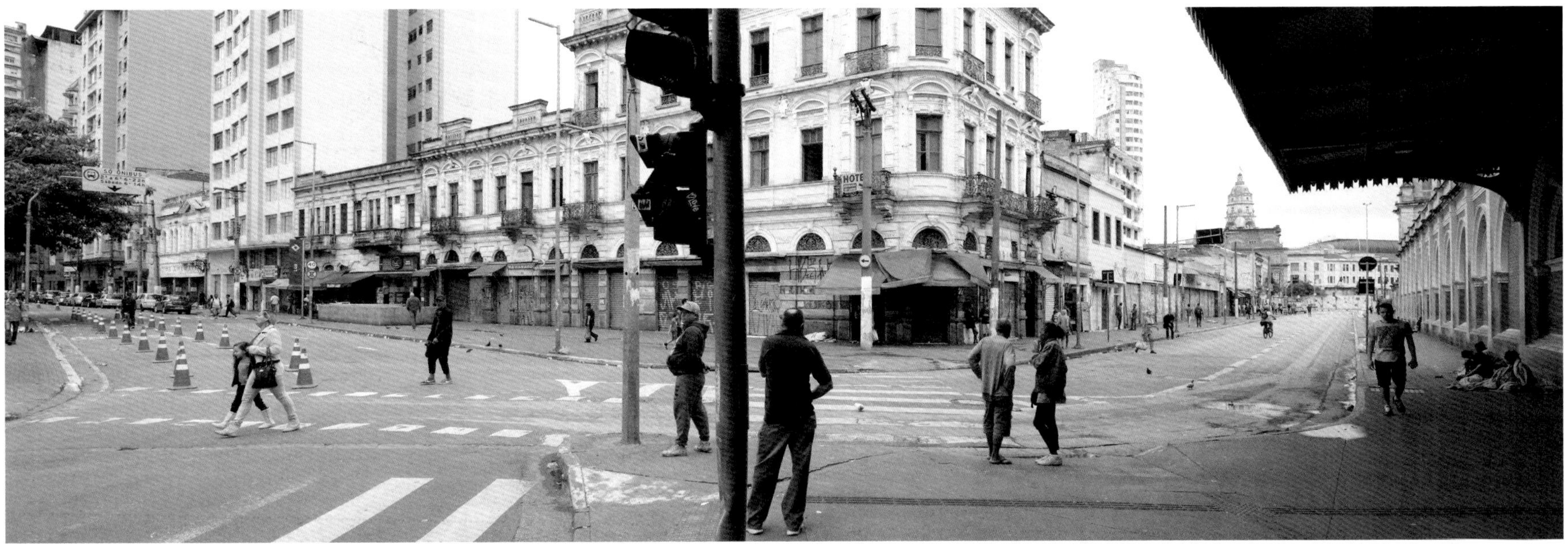

Sao Paulo 2018

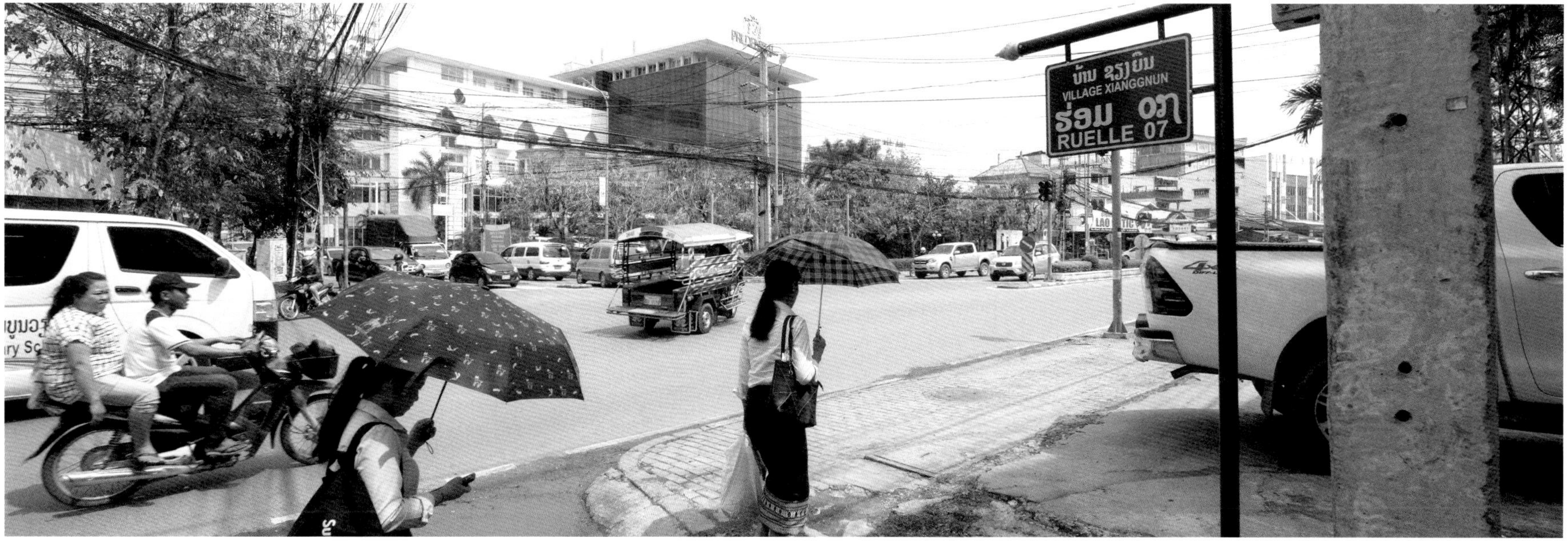
VILLAGE XIANGGNUN
RUELLE 07

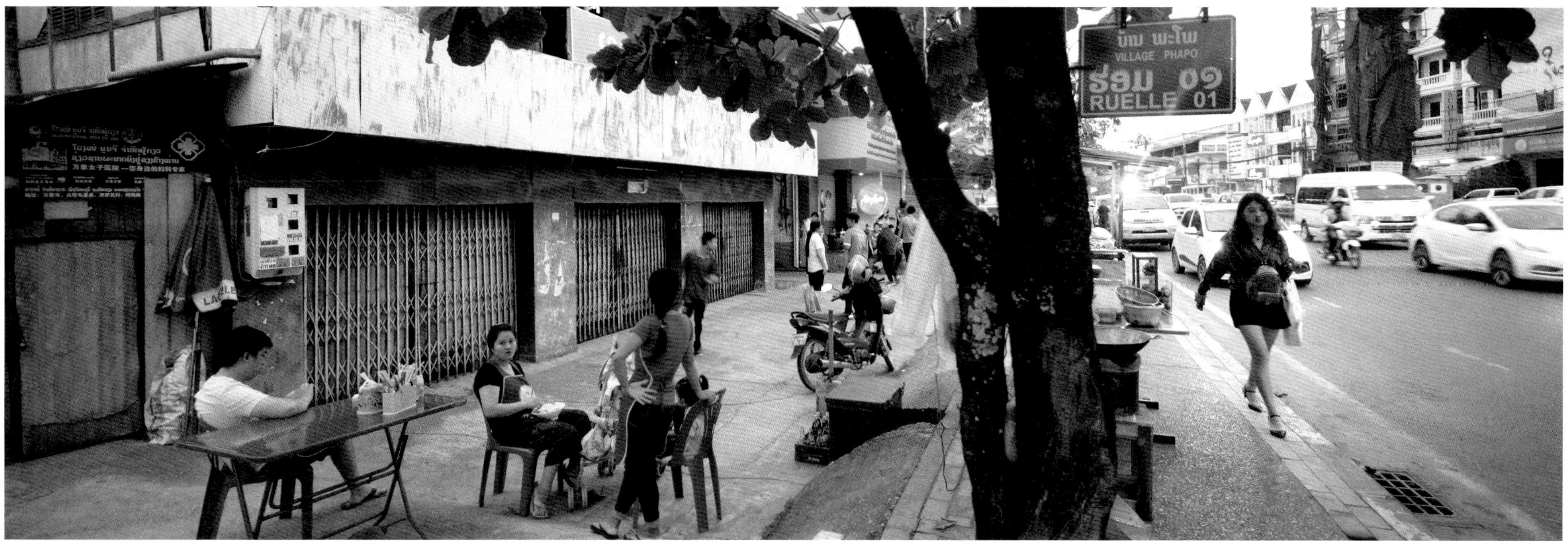
VILLAGE PHAPO
RUELLE 01

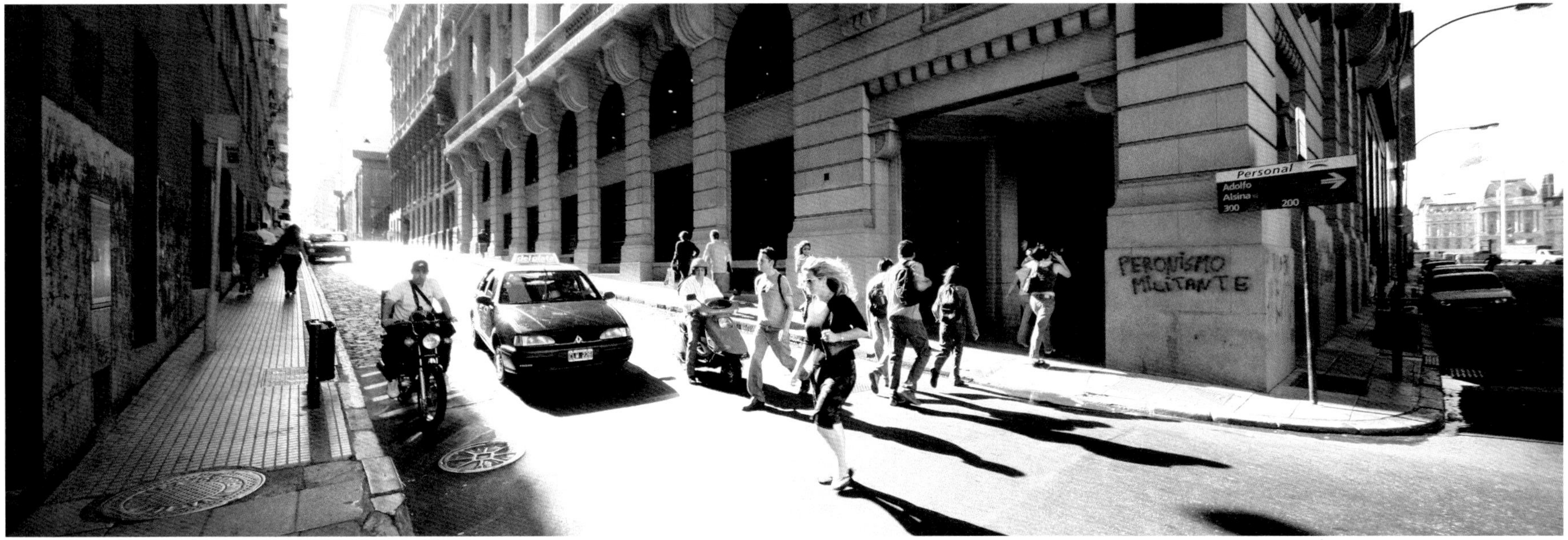

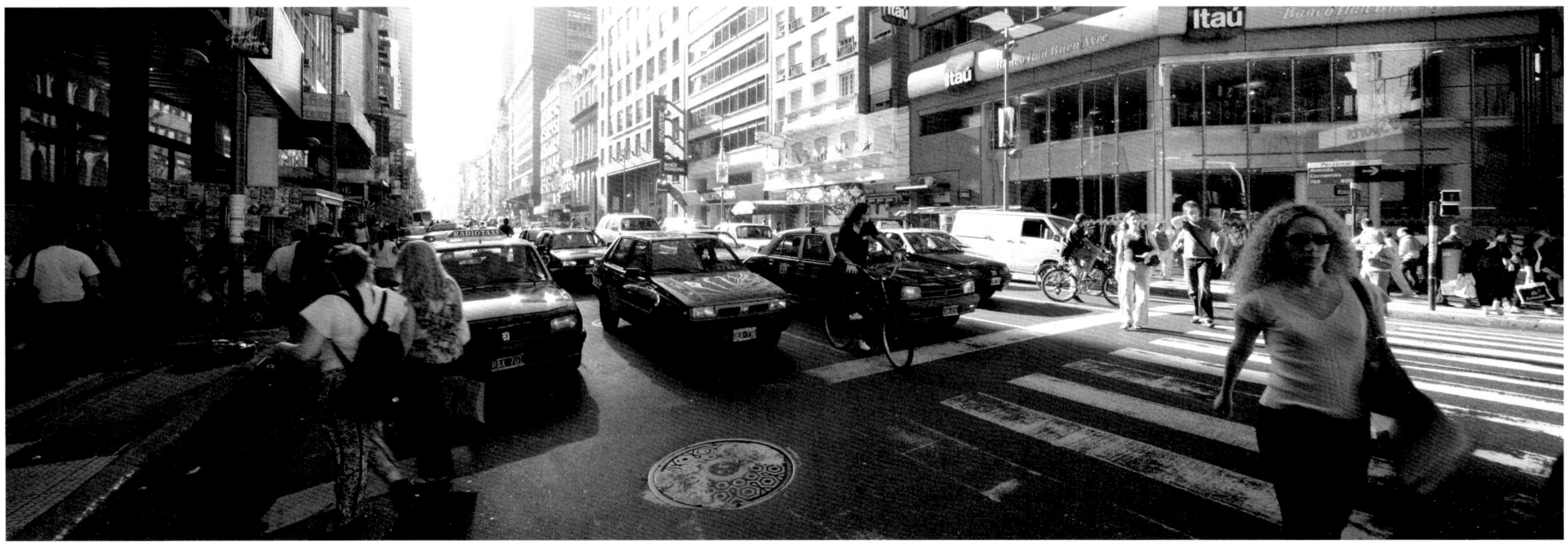

Buenos Aires 2005

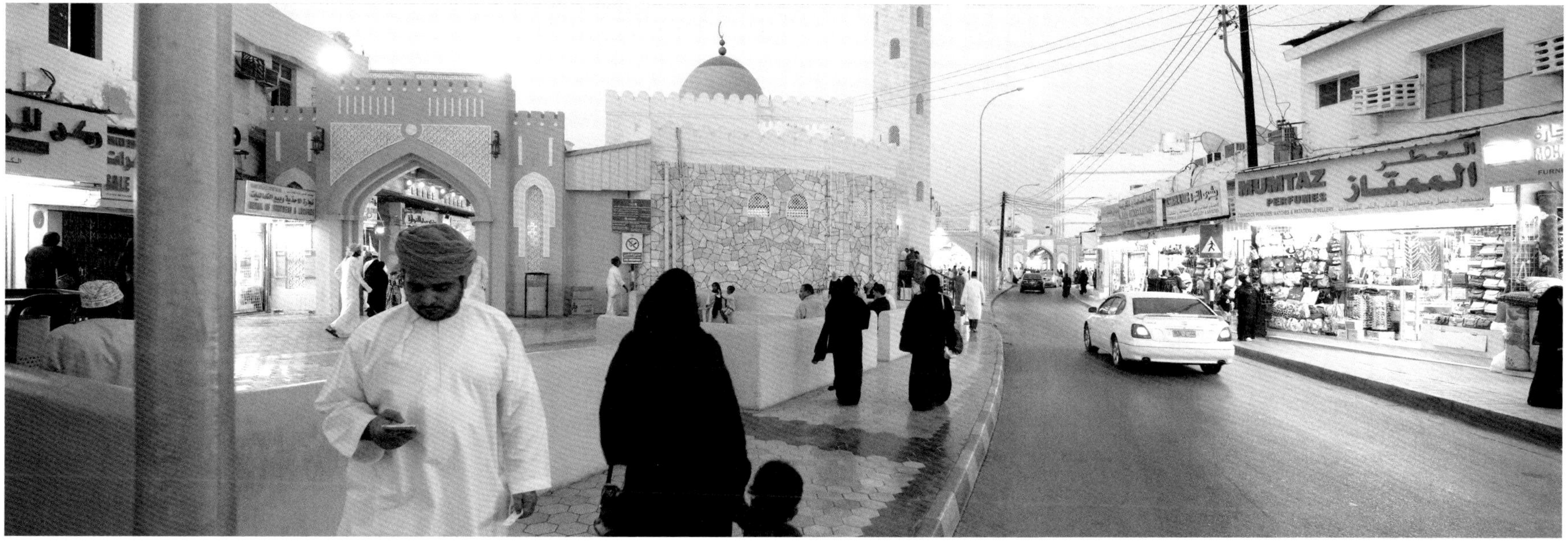
MUMTAZ
PERFUMES

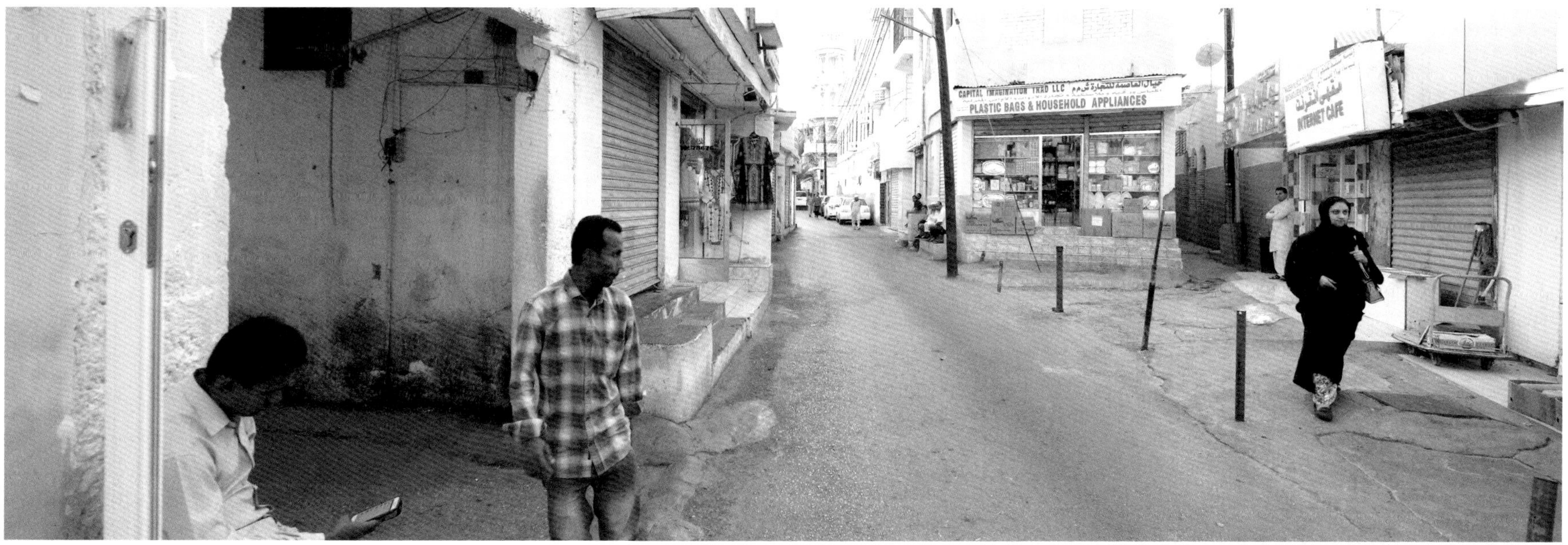
PLASTIC BAGS & HOUSEHOLD APPLIANCES
INTERNET CAFE

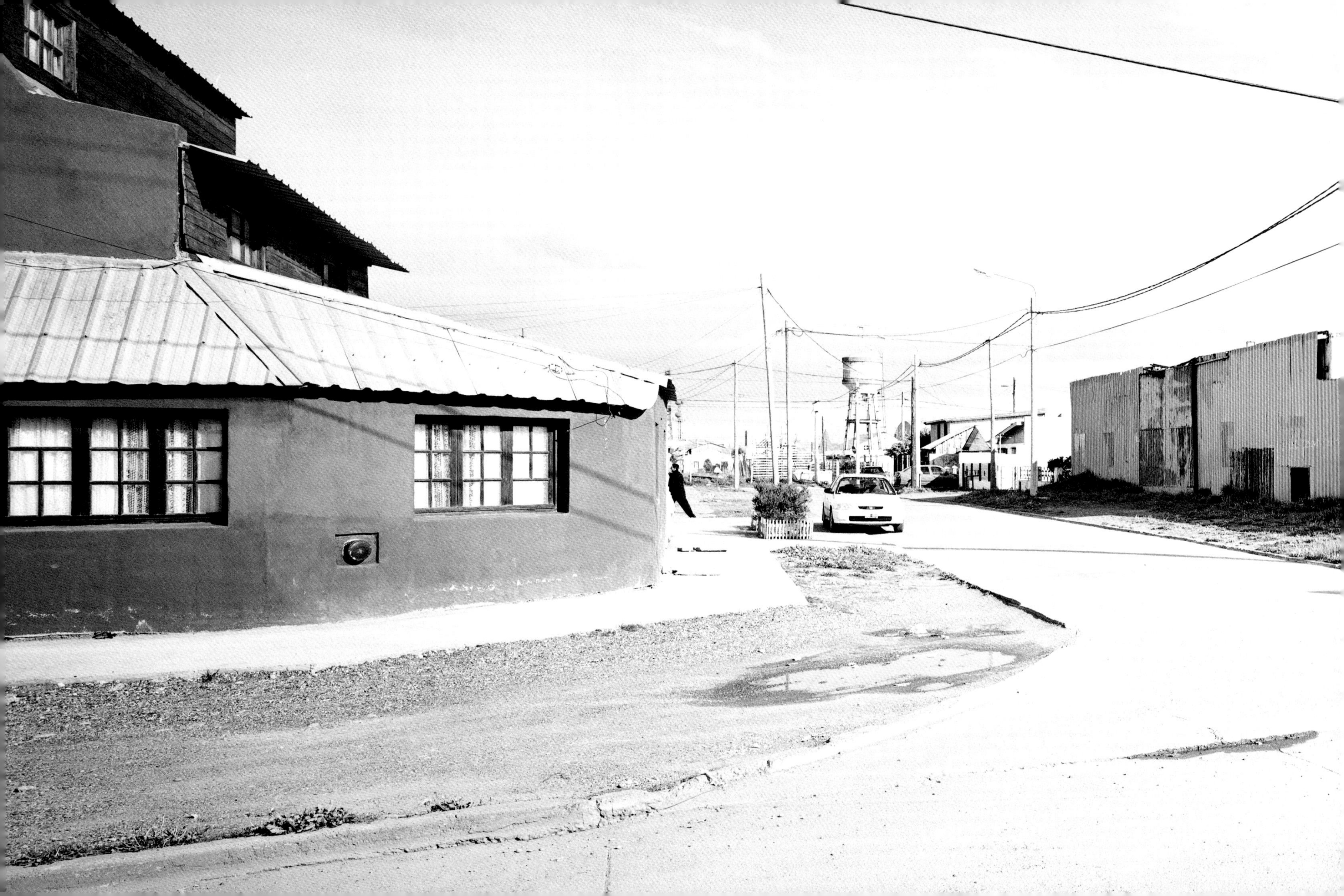

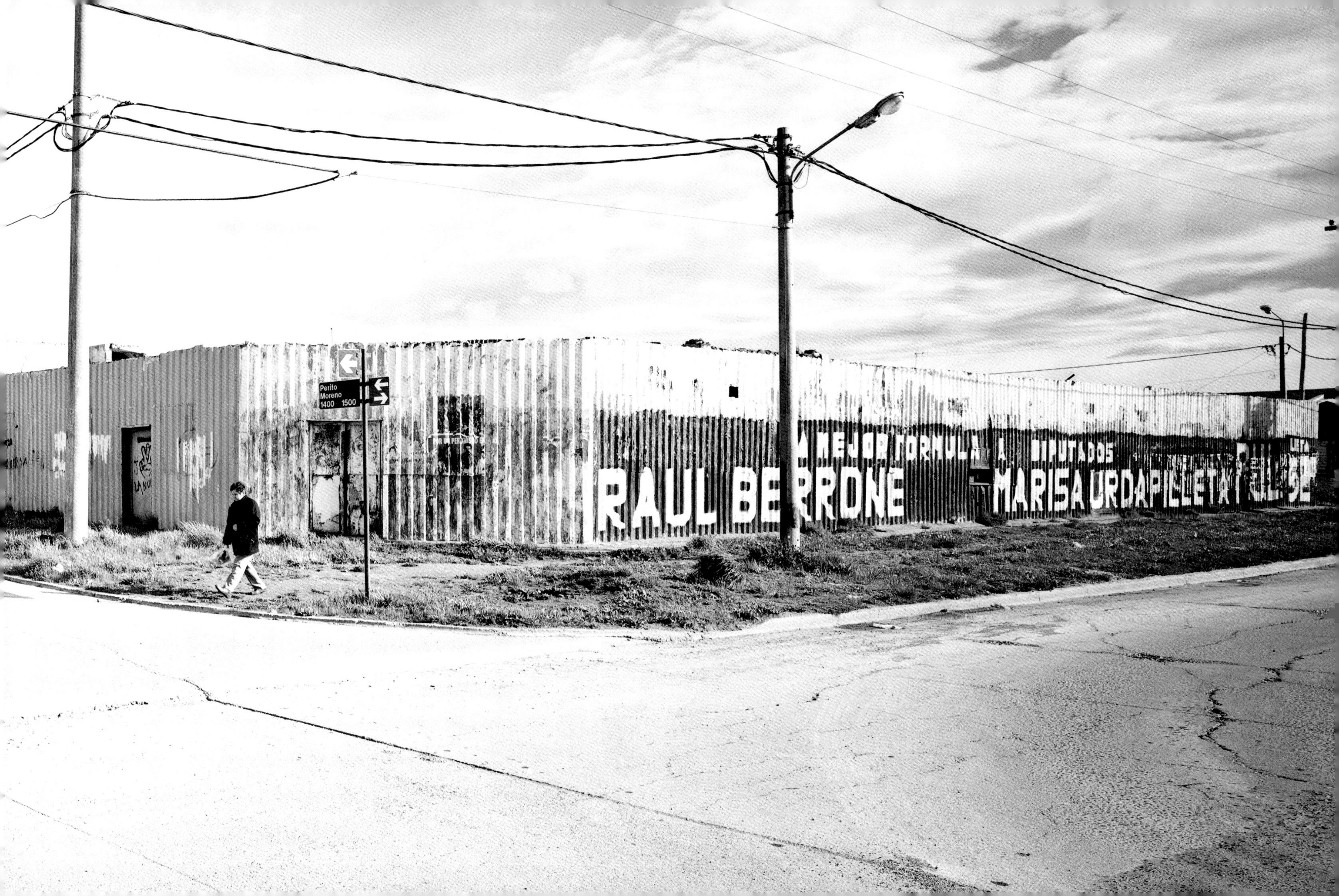
Perito Moreno
1400 1500
DIPUTADOS
RAUL
MARISA URDAPILLETA

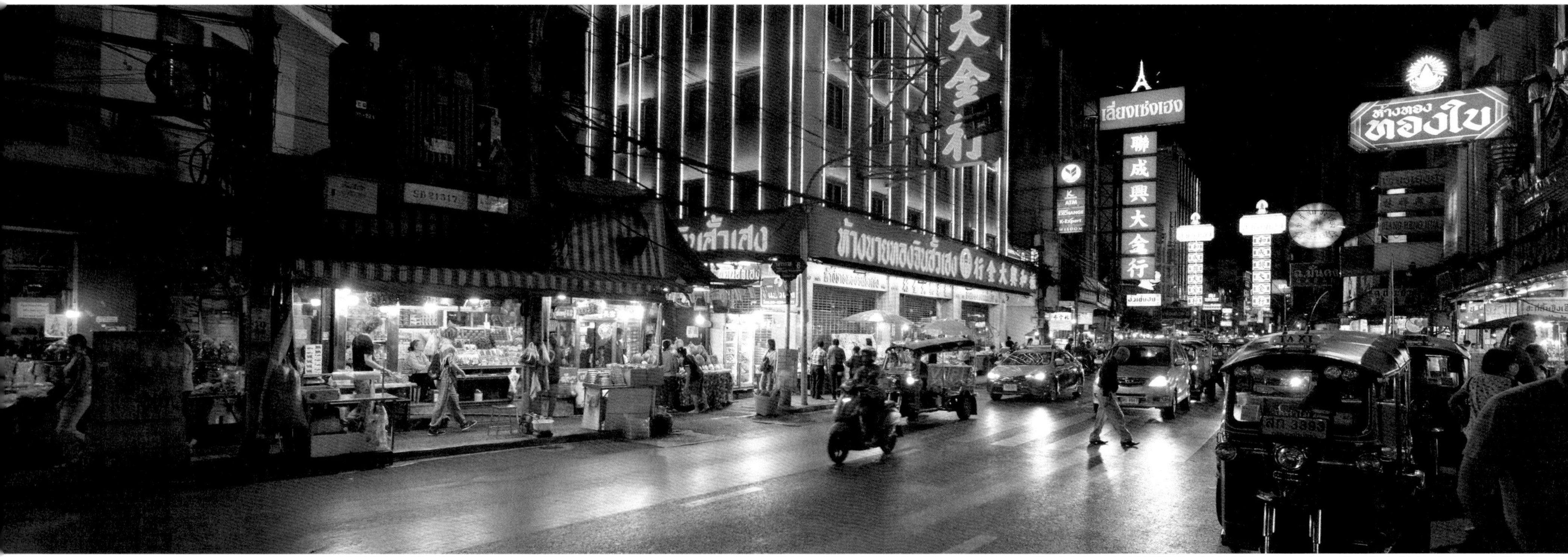

Bangkok 2019

< Rio Gallegos 2005